Strafford: An Historical Tragedy by Robert Browning

Robert Browning is one of the most significant Victorian Poets and, of course, English Poetry.

Much of his reputation is based upon his mastery of the dramatic monologue although his talents encompassed verse plays and even a well-regarded essay on Shelley during a long and prolific career.

He was born on May 7th, 1812 in Walmouth, London. Much of his education was home based and Browning was an eclectic and studious student, learning several languages and much else across a myriad of subjects, interests and passions.

Browning's early career began promisingly. The fragment from his intended long poem Pauline brought him to the attention of Dante Gabriel Rossetti, and was followed by Paracelsus, which was praised by both William Wordsworth and Charles Dickens. In 1840 the difficult Sordello, which was seen as willfully obscure, brought his career almost to a standstill.

Despite these artistic and professional difficulties his personal life was about to become immensely fulfilling. He began a relationship with, and then married, the older and better known Elizabeth Barrett. This new foundation served to energise his writings, his life and his career.

During their time in Italy they both wrote much of their best work. With her untimely death in 1861 he returned to London and thereafter began several further major projects.

The collection Dramatis Personae (1864) and the book-length epic poem The Ring and the Book (1868-69) were published and well received; his reputation as a venerated English poet now assured.

Robert Browning died in Venice on December 12th, 1889.

Index of Contents

DEDICATION

DEDICATED, IN ALL AFFECTIONATE ADMIRATION,
TO WILLIAM C. MACREADY, ESQ.

BY HIS MOST GRATEFUL AND DEVOTED FRIEND,

Robert Browning
April 23, 1837.

PREFACE

I had for some time been engaged in a Poem of a very different nature, when induced to make the present attempt; and am not without apprehension that my eagerness to freshen a jaded mind by diverting it to the healthy natures of a grand epoch, may have operated unfavourably on the represented play, which is one of Action in Character rather than Character in Action. To remedy this, in some degree, considerable curtailment will be necessary, and, in a few instances, the supplying details not required, I suppose, by the mere reader. While a trifling success would much gratify, failure will not wholly discourage me from another effort: experience is to come, and earnest endeavour may yet remove many disadvantages.

The portraits are, I think, faithful; and I am exceedingly fortunate in being able, in proof of this, to refer to the subtle and eloquent exposition of the characters of Eliot and Strafford, in the Lives of Eminent British Statesmen now in the course of publication in Lardner's Cyclopædia, by a writer whom I am proud to call my friend; and whose biographies of Hampden, Pym, and Vane, will, I am sure, fitly illustrate the present year—the Second Centenary of the Trial concerning Ship-Money. My Carlisle, however, is purely imaginary: I at first sketched her singular likeness roughly in, as suggested by Matthew and the memoir-writers—but it was too artificial, and the substituted outline is exclusively from Voiture and Waller.

The Italian boat-song in the last scene is from Redi's Bacco, long since naturalized in the joyous and delicate version of Leigh Hunt.

DRAMATIS PERSONÆ

Theatre-Royal Covent Garden, May 1, 1837

Charles the First	MR. DALE.
Earl of Holland	HUCKEL.
Lord Savile	TILBURY.
Sir Henry Vane	THOMPSON.
Wentworth, Viscount Wentworth, Earl of Strafford	MACREADY.
John Pym	VANDENHOFF.
John Hampden	HARRIS.
The younger Vane	J. WEBSTER.
Denzil Hollis	G. BENNET.
Benjamin Rudyard	PRITCHARD.
Nathaniel Fiennes	WORREL.
Earl of Loudon	BENDER.
Maxwell, Usher of the Black Rod	RANSFORD.
Balfour, Constable of the Tower	COLLETT.
A Puritan	WEBSTER.
Queen Henrietta	MISS VINCENT.
Lucy Percy, Countess of Carlisle	HELEN FAUCIT.

Presbyterians, Scots Commissioners, Adherents of Strafford, Secretaries, Officers of the Court &c. Two of Strafford's Children.

STRAFFORD

ACT I

SCENE I.—A HOUSE NEAR WHITEHALL

HAMPDEN, HOLLIS, the younger **VANE, RUDYARD, FIENNES,** and many of the Presbyterian Party: **LOUDON** and other Scots **COMMISSIONERS**: some seated, some standing beside a table strewn over with papers, &c.

VANE
I say, if he be here . . .

RUDYARD
And he is here!

HOLLIS
For England's sake let every man be still
Nor speak of him, so much as say his name,
Till Pym rejoin us! Rudyard—Vane—remember
One rash conclusion may decide our course
And with it England's fate—think—England's fate!
Hampden, for England's sake they should be still!

VANE

You say so, Hollis? well, I must be still!
It is indeed too bitter that one man—
Any one man . . .

RUDYARD

You are his brother, Hollis!

HAMPDEN

Shame on you, Rudyard! time to tell him that,
When he forgets the Mother of us all.

RUDYARD

Do I forget her?

HAMPDEN

—You talk idle hate
Against her foe: is that so strange a thing?
Is hating Wentworth all the help she needs?

A PURITAN

The Philistine strode, cursing as he went:
But David—five smooth pebbles from the brook
Within his scrip . . .

RUDYARD

—Be you as still as David!

FIENNES

Here's Rudyard not ashamed to wag a tongue
Stiff with ten years' disuse of Parliaments;
Why, when the last sate, Wentworth sate with us!

RUDYARD

Let's hope for news of them now he returns:
—But I'll abide Pym's coming.

VANE

Now by Heaven
They may be cool that can, silent that can,
Some have a gift that way: Wentworth is here—
Here—and the King's safe closeted with him
Ere this! and when I think on all that's past
Since that man left us—how his single arm
Roll'd back the good of England, roll'd it back
And set the woeful Past up in its place . . .

A PURITAN

Exalting Dagon where the Ark should be!

VANE

. . . How that man has made firm the fickle King
—Hampden, I will speak out!—in aught he feared
To venture on before; taught Tyranny
Her dismal trade, the use of all her tools,
To ply the scourge yet screw the gag so close
That strangled agony bleeds mute to death:
—How he turns Ireland to a private stage
For training infant villanies, new ways
Of wringing treasure out of tears and gore,
Unheard oppressions nourished in the dark
To try how much Man's nature can endure
—If he dies under it, what harm? if not . . .

FIENNES

Why, one more trick is added to the rest
Worth a King's knowing—

RUDYARD

—And what Ireland bears
England may learn to bear.

VANE

. . . How all this while
That man has set himself to one dear task,
The bringing Charles to relish more and more
Power . . .

RUDYARD

Power without law . . .

FIENNES

Power and blood too . .

VANE

. . . Can I be still?

HAMPDEN

For that you should be still.

VANE

Oh, Hampden, then and now! The year he left us
The People by its Parliament could wrest
The Bill of Rights from the reluctant King:
And now,—he'll find in an obscure small room
A stealthy gathering of great-hearted men

That take up England's cause: England is—here!

HAMPDEN
And who despairs of England?

RUDYARD
That do I
If Wentworth is to rule her. I am sick
To think her wretched masters, Hamilton,
The muckworm Cottington, the maniac Laud,
May yet be longed for back again. I say
I do despair.

VANE
And, Rudyard, I'll say this—
And, [Turning to the **REST**] all true men say after me! not loud—
But solemnly and as you'd say a prayer:
This Charles, who treads our England under foot,
Has just so much—it may be fear or craft—
As bids him pause at each fresh outrage; friends,
He needs some sterner hand to grasp his own,
Some voice to ask, "Why shrink?—am I not by?"
—A man that England loved for serving her,
Found in his heart to say, "I know where best
The iron heel shall bruise her, for she leans
Upon me when you trample." Witness, you!
But inasmuch as life is hard to take
From England . . .

MANY VOICES
Go on, Vane! 'Tis well said, Vane!

VANE
. . . Who has not so forgotten Runnymead . . .

VOICES
'Tis well and bravely spoken, Vane! Go on!

VANE
. . There are some little signs of late she knows
The ground no place for her! no place for her!
When the King beckons—and beside him stands
The same bad man once more, with the same smile,
And the same savage gesture! Now let England
Make proof of us.

VOICES
Strike him—the Renegade—

Haman—Ahithophel—

HAMPDEN [To the **SCOTS**]
Gentlemen of the North,
It was not thus the night your claims were urged,
And we pronounced the League and Covenant
Of Scotland to be England's cause as well!
Vane, there, sate motionless the whole night through.

VANE
Hampden . . .

FIENNES
Stay Vane!

LOUDON
Be patient, gallant Vane!

VANE
Mind how you counsel patience, Loudon! you
Have still a Parliament, and a brave League
To back it; you are free in Scotland still—
While we are brothers (as these hands are knit
So let our hearts be!)—hope's for England yet!
But know you why this Wentworth comes? to quench
This faintest hope? that he brings war with him?
Know you this Wentworth? What he dares?

LOUDON
Dear Vane,
We know—'tis nothing new . . .

VANE
And what's new, then,
In calling for his life? Why Pym himself . . .
You must have heard—ere Wentworth left our cause
He would see Pym first; there were many more
Strong on the People's side and friends of his,—
Eliot that's dead, Rudyard and Hampden here,
But Wentworth cared not for them; only, Pym
He would see—Pym and he were sworn, they say,
To live and die together—so they met
At Greenwich: Wentworth, you are sure, was long,
Specious enough, the devil's argument
Lost nothing in his lips; he'd have Pym own
A Patriot could not do a purer thing
Than follow in his track; they two combined
Could put down England. Well, Pym heard him out—

One glance—you know Pym's eye—one word was all:
"You leave us, Wentworth: while your head is on
I'll not leave you."

HAMPDEN
Has Pym left Wentworth, then?
Has England lost him? Will you let him speak,
Or put your crude surmises in his mouth?
Away with this! [To the rest] Will you have Pym or Vane?

VOICES
Wait Pym's arrival! Pym shall speak!

HAMPDEN
Meanwhile
Let Loudon read the Parliament's report
From Edinburgh: our last hope, as Vane says,
Is in the stand it makes. Loudon!

VANE [As **LOUDON** is about to read]
—No—no—
Silent I can be: not indifferent!

HAMPDEN
Then each keep silence, praying God a space
That he will not cast England quite away
In this her visitation!

[All assume a posture of reverence.

A PURITAN
Seven years long
The Midianite drove Israel into dens
And caves.
Till God sent forth a mighty man,

[**PYM** enters.

Even Gideon!

[All start up.

PYM
Wentworth's come: he has not reached
Whitehall: they've hurried up a Council there
To lose no time and find him work enough.
Where's Loudon? your Scots' Parliament . . .

LOUDON
Is firm:
We were about to read reports . . .

PYM
The King
Has just dissolved your Parliament.

LOUDON and other of the **SCOTS**
Great God!
An oath-breaker! Stand by us England then!

PYM
The King's too sanguine; doubtless Wentworth's here;
But still some little form might be kept up.

HOLLIS
Now speak, Vane! Rudyard, you had much to say!

HAMPDEN
The rumour's false, then . . .

PYM
Ay, the Court gives out
His own concerns have brought him back: I know
'Tis Charles recalls him: he's to supersede
The tribe of Cottingtons and Hamiltons
Whose part is played: there's talk enough, by this,—
Merciful talk, the King thinks: time is now
To turn the record's last and bloody leaf
That, chronicling a Nation's great despair,
Tells they were long rebellious, and their Lord
Indulgent, till, all kind expedients tried,
He drew the sword on them, and reigned in peace.
Laud's laying his religion on the Scots
Was the last gentle entry:—the new page
Shall run, the King thinks, "Wentworth thrust it down
At the sword's point."

A PURITAN
I'll do your bidding, Pym,—
England's and your's . . one blow!

PYM
A glorious thing—
We all say, friends, it is a glorious thing
To right that England! Heaven grows dark above,—
Let's snatch one moment ere the thunder fall

To say how well the English spirit comes out
Beneath it! all have done their best, indeed,
From lion Eliot, that grand Englishman,
To the least here: and who, the least one here,
When She is saved (and her redemption dawns
Dimly, most dimly, but it dawns—it dawns)—
Who'd give at any price his hope away
Of being named along with the Great Men?
One would not .. no, one would not give that up!

HAMPDEN
And one name shall be dearer than all names:
When children, yet unborn, are taught that name
After their fathers',—taught one matchless man . . .

PYM
. . . Saved England?
What if Wentworth's should be still
That name?

RUDYARD and **OTHERS**
We have just said it, Pym! His death
Saves her!

FIENNES
We said that! There's no way beside!

A PURITAN
I'll do your bidding, Pym! They struck down Joab
And purged the land.

VANE
No villanous striking-down!

RUDYARD
No—a calm vengeance: let the whole land rise
And shout for it. No Feltons!

PYM
Rudyard, no.
England rejects all Feltons; most of all
Since Wentworth . . .
Hampden, say the praise again
That England will award me . . . But I'll think
You know me, all of you. Then, I believe,
—Spite of the past,—Wentworth rejoins you, friends!

RUDYARD and **OTHERS**

Wentworth! apostate . . .

VANE
Wentworth, double-dyed
A traitor! Is it Pym, indeed . .

PYM
. . . Who says
Vane never knew that Wentworth—loved that Wentworth—
Felt glad to stroll with him, arm lock'd in arm,
Along the streets to see the People pass
And read in every island-countenance
Fresh argument for God against the King,—
Never sate down . . . say, in the very house
Where Eliot's brow grew broad with noble thoughts
(You've joined us, Hampden, Hollis, you as well.)
And then left talking over Gracchus' death . . .

VANE
. . To frame, we know it Pym, the choicest clause
In the Petition of Rights: which Wentworth framed
A month before he took at the King's hand
His Northern Presidency, which that Bill
Denounced. . . . .

RUDYARD
And infamy along with it!

A PURITAN
For whoso putteth his right-hand to the plough
And turneth back . . .

PYM
Never more, never more
Walked we together! Most alone I went;
I have had friends—all here are fast my friends—
But I shall never quite forget that friend!
[After a pause]
And yet it could not but be real in him!
You Vane, you Rudyard, have no right to trust
That Wentworth . . . O will no one hope with me?
—Vane—think you Wentworth will shed English blood
Like water?

A PURITAN
Ireland is Aceldama!

PYM

Will he turn Scotland to a hunting-ground
To please the King, now that he knows the King?
The People or the King? The People, Hampden,
Or the King . . . and that King—Charles! Will no one hope?

HAMPDEN
Pym, we do know you: you'll not set your heart
On any baseless thing: but say one deed
Of Wentworth's, since he left us . . .

[Shouting without.

VANE
Pym, he comes
And they shout for him!—Wentworth!—he's with Charles—
The king embracing him—now—as we speak . .
And he, to be his match in courtesies,
Taking the whole war's risk upon himself!—
Now—while you tell us here how changed he is—
Do you hear, Pym? The People shout for him!

FIENNES
We'll not go back, now! Hollis has no brother—
Vane has no father . . .

VANE
Pym should have no friend!
Stand you firm, Pym! Eliot's gone, Wentworth's lost,
We have but you, and stand you very firm!
Truth is eternal, come below what will,
But . . I know not . . if you should fail . . O God!
O God!

PYM [apart and in thought]
And yet if 'tis a dream, no more,
That Wentworth chose their side, and brought the King
To love it as though Laud had loved it first,
And the Queen after—that he led their cause
Calm to success and kept it spotless through,
So that our very eyes could look upon
The travail of our soul, and close content
That violence, which something mars even Right
That sanctions it, had taken off no grace
From its serene regard. Only a dream!

HAMPDEN
Proceed to England's work: who reads the list?

A VOICE
"Ship-money is refused or fiercely paid
In every county, save the northern ones
Where Wentworth's influence" . . .

[Renewed shouting.

VANE [passionately striking the table]
I, in England's name
Declare her work, this way, at end! till now—
Up to this moment—peaceful strife was well!
We English had free leave to think: till now,
We had a shadow of a Parliament:
'Twas well; but all is changed: they threaten us:
They'll try brute-force for law—here—in our land!

MANY VOICES
True hearts with Vane! The old true hearts with Vane!

VANE
Till we crush Wentworth for her, there's no act
Serves England!

VOICES
Vane for England!

PYM [As he passes slowly before them]
Pym should be
Something to England! I seek Wentworth, friends!

SCENE II.—WHITEHALL

Enter **CARLISLE** and **WENTWORTH**.

WENTWORTH
And the King?

CARLISLE
Dear Wentworth, lean on me; sit then;
I'll tell you all; this horrible fatigue
Will kill you.

WENTWORTH
No; or—Lucy, just your arm;
I'll not sit till I've cleared this up with him:
After that, rest. The King?

CARLISLE
Confides in you.

WENTWORTH
Why? why now?
—They have kind throats, the people!
Shout for me . . . they!—poor fellows.

CARLISLE
Did they shout?
—We took all measures to keep off the crowd—
Did they shout for you?

WENTWORTH
Wherefore should they not?
Does the King take such measures for himself?
Beside, there's such a dearth of malcontents,
You say?

CARLISLE
I said but few dared carp at you . . .

WENTWORTH
At me? at us, Carlisle! The King and I!
He's surely not disposed to let me bear
Away the fame from him of these late deeds
In Ireland? I am yet his instrument
Be it for well or ill?
He trusts me then?

CARLISLE
The King, dear Wentworth, purposes, I know
To grant you, in the face of all the Court . . .

WENTWORTH
All the Court! Evermore the Court about us!
Savile and Holland, Hamilton and Vane
About us,—then the King will grant me. . . . Lady,
Will the King leave these—leave all these—and say
"Tell me your whole mind, Wentworth!"

CARLISLE
But you said
You would be calm.

WENTWORTH
Lucy, and I am calm!

How else shall I do all I come to do,
—Broken, as you may see, body and mind—
How shall I serve the King? time wastes meanwhile,
You have not told me half . . . His footstep! No.
—But now, before I meet him,—(I am calm)—
Why does the King distrust me?

CARLISLE
He does not
Distrust you.

WENTWORTH
Lucy, you can help me . . you
Have even seemed to care for me: help me!
Is it the Queen?

CARLISLE
No—not the Queen—the party
That poisons the Queen's ear,—Savile—and Holland . . .

WENTWORTH
I know—I know—and Vane, too, he's one too?
Go on—and he's made Secretary—Well?
—Or leave them out and go straight to the charge!
The charge!

CARLISLE
O there's no charge—no precise charge—
Only they sneer, make light of . . . one may say
Nibble at what you do.

WENTWORTH
I know: but Lucy,
Go on, dear Lucy—Oh I need you so!
I reckoned on you from the first!—Go on!
. . Was sure could I once see this gentle girl
When I arrived, she'd throw an hour away
To help her weary friend . . .

CARLISLE
You thought of me,
Dear Wentworth?

WENTWORTH
. . But go on! The People here . . .

CARLISLE
They do not think your Irish Government

Of that surpassing value . . .

WENTWORTH
The one thing
Of value! The one service that the crown
May count on! All that keeps these very things
In power, to vex me . . .not that they do vex me,
Only it might vex some to hear that service
Decried—the sole support that's left the King!

CARLISLE
So the Archbishop says.

WENTWORTH
Ah? well, perhaps
The only hand held up in its defence
May be old Laud's!
These Hollands, then, these Saviles
Nibble? They nibble?—that's the very word!

CARLISLE
Your profit in the Customs, Bristol says, . . .

WENTWORTH
Enough! 'tis too unworthy,—I am not
So patient as I thought!
What's Pym about?

CARLISLE
Pym?

WENTWORTH
Pym and the People.

CARLISLE
Oh, the Faction!
Extinct—of no account—there'll never be
Another Parliament.

WENTWORTH
Tell Savile that!
You may know—(ay, you do—the creatures here
Never forget!) that in my earliest life
I was not . . . not what I am now! The King
May take my word on points concerning Pym
Before Lord Savile's, Lucy, or if not,
Girl, they shall ruin their vile selves, not me,
These Vanes and Hollands—I'll not be their tool—

Pym would receive me yet!
—But then the King!—
I'll bear it all. The King—where is he, Girl?

CARLISLE
He is apprised that you are here: be calm!

WENTWORTH
And why not meet me now? Ere now? You said
He sent for me . . he longed for me!

CARLISLE
Because . .
He is now . . . I think a Council's sitting now
About this Scots affair . . .

WENTWORTH
A Council sits?
They have not taken a decided course
Without me in this matter?

CARLISLE
I should say . . .

WENTWORTH
The War? They cannot have agreed to that?
Not the Scots' War?—without consulting me—
Me—that am here to show how rash it is,
How easy to dispense with?
—Ah, you too
Against me! well,—the King may find me here.

[As **CARLISLE** is going.

—Forget it, Lucy: cares make peevish: mine
Weigh me (but 'tis a secret) to my grave.

CARLISLE

For life or death I am your own, dear friend!
[Aside]
I could not tell him . . . sick too! . . And the King
Shall love him! Wentworth here, who can withstand
His look?—And he did really think of me?
O 'twas well done to spare him all the pain!

[Exit.

WENTWORTH

Heartless! . . . but all are heartless here.
Go now,
Forsake the people!
—I did not forsake
The People: they shall know it . . . when the King
Will trust me!—who trusts all beside at once
While I . . . have not spoke Vane and Savile fair,
And am not trusted: have but saved the Throne:
Have not picked up the Queen's glove prettily,
And am not trusted!
But he'll see me now:
And Weston's dead—and the Queen's English now—
More English—oh, one earnest word will brush
These reptiles from . . .

[Footsteps within.

The step I know so well!
'Tis Charles!—But now—to tell him . . no—to ask him
What's in me to distrust:—or, best begin
By proving that this frightful Scots affair
Is just what I foretold: I'll say, "my liege" . . . .
And I feel sick, now! and the time is come—
And one false step no way to be repaired. . . .
You were revenged, Pym, could you look on me!

[**PYM** enters.

WENTWORTH

I little thought of you just then.

PYM

No? I
Think always of you, Wentworth.

WENTWORTH [Aside]

The old voice!
I wait the King, sir.

PYM

True—you look so pale;
A council sits within; when that breaks up
He'll see you.

WENTWORTH

Sir, I thank you.

PYM
Oh, thank Laud!
You know when Laud once gets on Church affairs
The case is desperate: he'll not be long
To-day: He only means to prove, to-day,
We English all are mad to have a hand
In butchering the Scots for serving God
After their fathers' fashion: only that.

WENTWORTH
Sir, keep your jests for those who relish them!
[Aside]
Does he enjoy their confidence? [To **PYM**] 'Tis kind
To tell me what the Council does.

PYM
You grudge
That I should know it had resolved on war
Before you came? no need—you shall have all
The credit, trust me.

WENTWORTH
Have they, Pym . . . not dared—
They have not dared . . . that is—I know you not—
Farewell—the times are changed.

PYM
—Since we two met
At Greenwich? Yes—poor patriots though we be,
You shall see something here, some slight return
For your exploits in Ireland! Changed indeed,
Could our friend Eliot look from out his grave!
Ah, Wentworth, one thing for acquaintance-sake;
Just to decide a question; have you, now,
Really felt well since you forsook us?

WENTWORTH
Pym—
You're insolent!

PYM
Oh, you misapprehend!
Don't think I mean the advantage is with me:
I was about to say that, for my part,
I've never quite held up my head since then,—
Been quite myself since then: for first, you see,
I lost all credit after that event
With those who recollect how sure I was

Wentworth would outdo Eliot on our side.

WENTWORTH
By Heaven . . .

PYM
Forgive me: Savile, Vane, and Holland
Eschew plain-speaking: 'tis a trick I have.

WENTWORTH
How, when, where,—Savile, Vane, and Holland speak,—
Plainly or otherwise,—would have my scorn,
My perfect scorn, Sir . . .

PYM
. . Did not my poor thoughts
Claim somewhat?

WENTWORTH
Keep your thoughts! believe the King
Mistrusts me for their speaking, all these Vanes
And Saviles! make your mind up, all of you,
That I am discontented with the King!

PYM
Why, you may be—I should be, that I know,
Were I like you.

WENTWORTH
Like me?

PYM
I care not much
For titles: our friend Eliot died no Lord,
Hampden's no Lord, and Savile is a Lord:
But you care, since you sold your soul for one.
I can't think, therefore, Charles did well to laugh
When you twice prayed so humbly for an Earldom.

WENTWORTH
Pym. . . .

PYM
And your letters were the movingest!
Console yourself: I've borne him prayers just now
From Scotland not to be opprest by Laud—
And moving in their way: he'll pay, be sure,
As much attention as to those you sent.

WENTWORTH
False! a lie, Sir!
. . Who told you, Pym?
—But then
The King did very well . . nay, I was glad
When it was shewn me why;—I first refused it!
. . . Pym, you were once my friend—don't speak to me!

PYM
Oh, Wentworth, ancient brother of my soul,
That all should come to this!

WENTWORTH
Leave me!

PYM
My friend,
Why should I leave you?

WENTWORTH
To tell Rudyard this,
And Hampden this! . . .

PYM
Whose faces once were bright
At my approach . . now sad with doubt and fear,
Because I hope in you—Wentworth—in you
Who never mean to ruin England—you
Who shake, with God's great help, this frightful dream
Away, now, in this Palace, where it crept
Upon you first, and are yourself—your good
And noble self—our Leader—our dear Chief—
Hampden's own friend—
This is the proudest day!
Come Wentworth! Do not even see the King!
The rough old room will seem itself again!
We'll both go in together—you've not seen
Hampden so long—come—and there's Vane—I know
You'll love young Vane! This is the proudest day!

[The **KING** enters. **WENTWORTH** lets fall **PYM'S** hand.

CHARLES
Arrived, my Lord?—This Gentleman, we know,
Was your old friend:
[To **PYM**]
The Scots shall be informed

What we determine for their happiness.

[Exit **PYM**.

You have made haste, my Lord.

WENTWORTH
Sire . . . I am come . . .

CHARLES
To aid us with your counsel: this Scots' League
And Covenant spreads too far, and we have proofs
That they intrigue with France: the Faction, too . . .

WENTWORTH [Kneels]
Sire, trust me! but for this once, trust me, Sire!

CHARLES
What can you mean?

WENTWORTH
That you should trust me! now!
Oh—not for my sake! but 'tis sad, so sad
That for distrusting me, you suffer—you
Whom I would die to serve: Sire, do you think
That I would die to serve you?

CHARLES
But rise, Wentworth!

WENTWORTH
What shall convince you? What does Savile do
To . . . Ah, one can't tear out one's heart—one's heart—
And show it, how sincere a thing it is!

CHARLES
Have I not trusted you?

WENTWORTH
Say aught but that!
It is my comfort, mark you: all will be
So different when you trust me . . as you shall!
It has not been your fault,—I was away,
Maligned—away—and how were you to know?
I am here, now—you mean to trust me, now—
All will go on so well!

CHARLES

Be sure I will—
I've heard that I should trust you: as you came
Even Carlisle was telling me . . . .

WENTWORTH
No,—hear nothing—
Be told nothing about me! you're not told
Your right-hand serves you, or your children love you!

CHARLES
You love me . . . only rise!

WENTWORTH
I can speak now.
I have no right to hide the truth. 'Tis I
Can save you; only I. Sire, what is done!

CHARLES
Since Laud's assured . . . the minutes are within . .
Loath as I am to spill my subjects' blood . . . .

WENTWORTH
That is, he'll have a war: what's done is done!

CHARLES
They have intrigued with France; that's clear to Laud.

WENTWORTH
Has Laud suggested any way to meet
The war's expence?

CHARLES
He'd not decide on that
Until you joined us.

WENTWORTH
Most considerate!
You're certain they intrigue with France, these Scots?
[Aside]
The People would be with us!

CHARLES
Very sure.

WENTWORTH
(The People for us . . were the People for us!)
Sire, a great thought comes to reward your trust!
Summon a parliament! in Ireland first,

And then in England.

CHARLES
Madness!

WENTWORTH [Aside]
That puts off
The war—gives time to learn their grievances—
To talk with Pym—
[To **CHARLES**]
I know the faction, as
They style it, . .

CHARLES
. . Tutors Scotland!

WENTWORTH
All their plans
Suppose no parliament: in calling one
You take them by surprise. Produce the proofs
Of Scotland's treason; bid them help you, then!
Even Pym will not refuse!

CHARLES
You would begin
With Ireland?

WENTWORTH
Take no care for that: that's sure
To prosper.

CHARLES
You shall rule me: you were best
Return at once: but take this ere you go!

[Giving a paper.

Now, do I trust you? You're an Earl: my Friend
Of Friends: yes, Strafford, while . . . You hear me not!

WENTWORTH
Say it all o'er again—but once again—
The first was for the music—once again!

CHARLES
Strafford, my brave friend, there were wild reports—
Vain rumours . . . Henceforth touching Strafford is
To touch the apple of my sight: why gaze

So earnestly?

WENTWORTH
I am grown young again,
And foolish! . . what was it we spoke of?

CHARLES
Ireland,
The Parliament,—

WENTWORTH
I may go when I will?
—Now?

CHARLES
Are you tired so soon of me?

WENTWORTH
My King . . . .
But you will not so very much dislike
A Parliament? I'd serve you any way!

CHARLES
You said just now this was the only way.

WENTWORTH
Sire, I will serve you!

CHARLES
Strafford, spare yourself—
You are so sick, they tell me . . .

WENTWORTH
'Tis my soul
That's well and happy, now!
This Parliament—
We'll summon it, the English one—I'll care
For every thing: You shall not need them much!

CHARLES
If they prove restive . . .

WENTWORTH
I shall be with you!

CHARLES
Ere they assemble?

WENTWORTH
I will come, or else
Deposit this infirm humanity
I'the dust! My whole heart stays with you, my King!

[As **STRAFFORD** goes out, the **QUEEN** enters.

CHARLES
That man must love me!

QUEEN
Is it over then?
Why he looks yellower than ever! well,
At least we shall not hear eternally
Of his vast services: he's paid at last.

CHARLES
Not done with: he engages to surpass
All yet performed in Ireland.

QUEEN
I had thought
Nothing beyond was ever to be done.
The War, Charles—will he raise supplies enough?

CHARLES
We've hit on an expedient; he . . . that is,
I have advised . . . we have decided on
The calling—in Ireland—of a Parliament.

QUEEN
O truly! You agree to that? Is this
The first fruit of his counsel? But I guessed
As much.

CHARLES
This is too idle, Henrietta!
I should know best: He will strain every nerve,
And once a precedent established . . .

QUEEN
Notice
How sure he is of a long term of favours!
He'll see the next, and the next after that;
No end to Parliaments!

CHARLES
Well, it is done:

He talks it smoothly, doubtless: if, indeed,
The Commons here . . .

QUEEN
Here! you will summon them
Here? Would I were in France again to see
A King!

CHARLES
But Henrietta . . .

QUEEN
O the Scots
Do well to spurn your rule!

CHARLES
But, listen, Sweet . . .

QUEEN
Let Strafford listen—you confide in him!

CHARLES
I do not, Love—I do not so confide . .
The Parliament shall never trouble us
. . Nay, hear me! I have schemes—such schemes—we'll buy
The leaders off: without that, Strafford's counsel
Had ne'er prevailed on me. Perhaps I call it
To have excuse for breaking it—for ever—
And whose will then the blame be? See you not?
Come, Dearest!—look! the little fairy, now,
That cannot reach my shoulder! Dearest, come!

[Exeunt.

ACT II

SCENE I.—As in Act I. Scene I

The same Party enters confusedly; among the first, the younger **VANE** and **RUDYARD**

RUDYARD
Twelve subsidies!

VANE
O Rudyard, do not laugh
At least!

RUDYARD
True: Strafford called the Parliament—
'Tis he should laugh!

A PURITAN [entering]
—Out of the serpent's root
Comes forth a cockatrice.

FIENNES [entering]
—A stinging one,
If that's the Parliament: twelve subsidies!
A stinging one! but, brother, where's your word
For Strafford's other nest-egg—the Scot's War?

THE PURITAN
His fruit shall be a fiery flying serpent.

FIENNES
Shall be? It chips the shell, man; peeps abroad:
Twelve subsidies!—
Why, how now Vane?

RUDYARD
Hush, Fiennes!

FIENNES
Ah? . . . but he was not more a dupe than I,
Or you, or any here the day that Pym
Returned with the good news. Look up, dear Vane!
We all believed that Strafford meant us well
In summoning the Parliament . . .

[**HAMPDEN** enters.

VANE [starting up]
Now, Hampden,
Clear me! I would have leave to sleep again!
I'd look the People in the face again!
Clear me from having, from the first, hoped, dreamed
Better of Strafford! Fool!

HAMPDEN
You'll grow one day
A steadfast light to England, Vane!

RUDYARD
Ay, Fiennes,

Strafford revived our Parliaments: before,
War was but talked of; there's an army, now:
Still, we've a Parliament. Poor Ireland bears
Another wrench (she dies the hardest death!)
Why . . . speak of it in Parliament! and, lo,
'Tis spoken!—and console yourselves.

FIENNES
The jest!
We clamoured, I suppose, thus long, to win
The privilege of laying on ourselves
A sorer burthen than the King dares lay!

RUDYARD
Mark now: we meet at length: complaints pour in
From every county: all the land cries out
On loans and levies, curses ship-money,
Calls vengeance on the Star-chamber: we lend
An ear: "ay, lend them all the ears you have,"
Puts in the King; "my subjects, as you find,
Are fretful, and conceive great things of you:
Just listen to them, friends: you'll sanction me
The measures they most wince at, make them yours
Instead of mine, I know: and, to begin,
They say my levies pinch them,—raise me straight
Twelve subsidies!"

FIENNES and **OTHERS**
All England cannot furnish
Twelve subsidies!

HOLLIS
But Strafford, just returned
From Ireland . . what has he to do with that?
How could he speak his mind? He left before
The Parliament assembled: Rudyard, friends,
He could not speak his mind! and Pym, who knows
Strafford . . .

RUDYARD
Would I were sure we know ourselves!
What is for good, what, bad—who friend, who foe!

HOLLIS
Do you count Parliaments no gain?

RUDYARD
A gain?

While the King's creatures overbalance us?
—There's going on, beside, among ourselves
A quiet, slow, but most effectual course
Of buying over, sapping, . .

A PURITAN
. . Leavening
The lump till all is leaven.

A VOICE
Glanville's gone.

RUDYARD
I'll put a case; had not the Court declared
That no sum short of just twelve subsidies
Will be accepted by the King—our House
Would have consented to that wretched offer
To let us buy off Ship-money?

HOLLIS
Most like,
If . . . say six subsidies, will buy it off,
The House. . . .

RUDYARD
. . Will grant them! Hampden, do you hear?
Oh, I congratulate you that the King
Has gained his point at last . . our own assent
To that detested tax! all's over then!
There's no more taking refuge in this room
And saying, "Let the King do what he will,
We, England, are no party to our shame,—
Our day will come!" Congratulate with me!

[**PYM** enters.

VANE
Pym, Strafford called this Parliament, 'tis like—
But we'll not have our Parliaments like those
In Ireland, Pym!

RUDYARD
Let him stand forth, that Strafford!
One doubtful act hides far too many sins;
It can be stretched no more—and, to my mind,
Begins to drop from those it covers.

OTHER VOICES

Pym,
Let him avow himself! No fitter time!
We wait thus long for you!

RUDYARD
Perhaps, too long!
Since nothing but the madness of the Court
In thus unmasking its designs at once
Had saved us from betraying England. Stay—
This Parliament is Strafford's: let us vote
Our list of grievances too black by far
To suffer talk of subsidies: or best—
That Ship-money's disposed of long ago
By England; any vote that's broad enough:
And then let Strafford, for the love of it,
Support his Parliament!

VANE
And vote as well
No war's to be with Scotland! Hear you, Pym?
We'll vote, no War! No part nor lot in it
For England!

MANY VOICES
Vote, no War! Stop the new levies!
No Bishop's War! At once! When next we meet!

PYM
Much more when next we meet!
—Friends, which of you
Since first the course of Strafford was in doubt
Has fallen the most away in soul from me?

VANE
I sate apart, even now, under God's eye,
Pondering the words that should denounce you, Pym,
In presence of us all, as one at league
With England's enemy!

PYM
You are a good
And gallant spirit, Henry! Take my hand
And say you pardon me for all the pain
Till now! Strafford is wholly ours.

MANY VOICES
'Tis sure?

PYM

Most sure—for Charles dissolves the Parliament
While I speak here! . . .

[Great emotion in the assembly.

. . And I must speak, friends, now!
Strafford is ours! The King detects the change,
Casts Strafford off for ever, and resumes
His ancient path: no Parliament for us—
No Strafford for the King!
Come all of you
To bid the King farewell, predict success
To his Scots expedition, and receive
Strafford, our comrade now! The next will be
Indeed a Parliament!

VANE

Forgive me, Pym!

VOICES

This looks like truth—Strafford can have, indeed,
No choice!

PYM

Friends, follow me! he's with the King:
Come Hampden, and come Rudyard, and come Vane—
This is no sullen day for England, Vane!
Strafford shall tell you!

VOICES

To Whitehall then! Come!

[Exeunt **OMNES**.

SCENE II.—WHITEHALL

CHARLES seated, **STRAFFORD** standing beside a table covered with maps, &c.

CHARLES

Strafford . . .

STRAFFORD

Is it a dream? my papers, here—
Thus—as I left them—all the plans you found
So happy—(look! The track you pressed my hand

For pointing out!)—and in this very room
Over these very plans, you tell me, Sire,
With the same face, too,—tell me just one thing
That ruins them! How's this? what may this mean?
Sire, who has done this?

CHARLES
Strafford, none but I!
You bade me put the rest away—indeed
You are alone!

STRAFFORD
Alone—and like to be!
No fear, when some unworthy scheme's grown ripe,
Of those who hatched it leaving you to loose
The mischief on the world! Laud hatches war,
Falls to his prayers, and leaves the rest to me—
And I'm alone!

CHARLES
At least, you knew as much
When first you undertook the war.

STRAFFORD
My liege,
Is this the way? I said, since Laud would lap
A little blood, 'twere best to hurry o'er
The loathsome business—not to be whole months
At slaughter—one blow—only one—then, peace—
Save for the dreams! I said, to please you both
I'd lead an Irish Army to the West,
While in the South the English . . . . . but you look
As though you had not told me fifty times
'Twas a brave plan! My Army is all raised—
I am prepared to join it . . .

CHARLES
Hear me, Strafford!

STRAFFORD
. . . When, for some little thing, my whole design
Is set aside—(where is the wretched paper?)
I am to lead—(ay, here it is)—to lead
This English Army: why? Northumberland
That I appointed, chooses to be sick—
Is frightened: and, meanwhile, who answers for
The Irish Parliament? or Army, either?
Is this my plan? I say, is this my plan?

CHARLES
You are disrespectful, Sir!

STRAFFORD
Do not believe—
My liege, do not believe it! I am yours—
Yours ever—'tis too late to think about—
To the death, yours! Elsewhere, this untoward step
Shall pass for mine—the world shall think it mine—
But, here! But, here! I am so seldom here!
Seldom with you, my King! I—soon to rush
Alone—upon a Giant—in the dark!

CHARLES
My Strafford!

STRAFFORD [Seats himself at the table; examines papers awhile; then, breaking off]
.. "Seize the passes of the Tyne" . . .
But don't you see—see all I say is true?
My plan was sure to prosper,—so, no cause
To ask the Parliament for help; whereas
We need them—frightfully . . .

CHARLES
Need this Parliament?

STRAFFORD
—Now, for God's sake, mind—not one error more!
We can afford no error—we draw, now,
Upon our last resource—this Parliament
Must help us!

CHARLES
I've undone you, Strafford!

STRAFFORD
Nay—
Nay—don't despond—Sire—'tis not come to that!
I have not hurt you? Sire—what have I said
To hurt you? I'll unsay it! Don't despond!
Sire, do you turn from me?

CHARLES
My friend of friends!

STRAFFORD [after a pause]
We'll make a shift! Leave me the Parliament!

They help us ne'er so little but I'll make
A vast deal out of it. We'll speak them fair:
They're sitting: that's one great thing: that half gives
Their sanction to us: that's much: don't despond!
Why, let them keep their money, at the worst!
The reputation of the People's help
Is all we want: we'll make shift yet!

CHARLES
Dear Strafford!

STRAFFORD
But meantime, let the sum be ne'er so small
They offer, we'll accept it: any sum—
For the look of it: the least grant tells the Scots
The Parliament is ours . . their staunch ally
Is ours: that told, there's scarce a blow to strike!
What will the grant be? What does Glanville think?

CHARLES
Alas . . .

STRAFFORD
My liege?

CHARLES
Strafford . . .

STRAFFORD
But answer me!
Have they . . . O surely not refused us all?
All the twelve subsidies? We never looked
For all of them! How many do they give?

CHARLES
You have not heard . . .

STRAFFORD
(What has he done?)—Heard what?
But speak at once, Sire—this grows terrible!

[The **KING** continuing silent.

You have dissolved them!—I'll not leave this man.

CHARLES
'Twas Vane—his ill-judged vehemence that . . .

STRAFFORD
Vane?

CHARLES
He told them, as they were about to vote
The half, that nothing short of all the twelve
Would serve our turn, or be accepted.

STRAFFORD
Vane!
Vane! and you promised me that very Vane . . .
O God, to have it gone, quite gone from me
The one last hope—I that despair, my hope—
That I should reach his heart one day, and cure
All bitterness one day, be proud again
And young again, care for the sunshine too,
And never think of Eliot any more,—
God, and to toil for this, go far for this,
Get nearer, and still nearer, reach this heart—
And find Vane there!

[Suddenly taking up a paper, and continuing with a forced calmness.

Northumberland is sick:
Well then, I take the Army: Wilmot leads
The Horse, and he with Conway must secure
The passes of the Tyne: Ormond supplies
My place in Ireland. Here, we'll try the City:
If they refuse a loan . . . debase the coin
And seize the bullion! we've no other choice.
Herbert . . .

[Flinging down the paper.

And this while I am here! with you!
And there are hosts such, hosts like Vane! I go,—
And, I once gone, they'll close around you, Sire,
When the least pique, pettiest mistrust, is sure
To ruin me—and you along with me!
Do you see that? And you along with me!
—Sire, you'll not ever listen to these men,
And I away, fighting your battle? Sire,
If they—if She—charge me—no matter what—
You say, "At any time when he returns
His head is mine." Don't stop me there! You know
My head is yours . . only, don't stop me there!

CHARLES

Too shameful, Strafford! You advised the war,
And . . .

STRAFFORD
I! I! that was never spoken with
Till it was entered on! That loathe the war!
That say it is the maddest, wickedest . . .
Do you know, Charles, I think, within my heart,
That you would say I did advise the war;
And if, thro' your own weakness, falsehood, Charles,
These Scots, with God to help them, drive me back . . .
You will not step between the raging People
And me, to say . . .
I knew you! from the first
I knew you! Never was so cold a heart!
Remember that I said it—that I never
Believed you for a moment!
—And, you loved me?
You thought your perfidy profoundly hid
Because I could not share your whisperings
With Vane? With Savile? But your hideous heart—
I had your heart to see, Charles! Oh, to have
A heart of stone—of smooth, cold, frightful stone!
Ay, call them! Shall I call for you? The Scots
Goaded to madness? Or the English—Pym—
Shall I call Pym, your subject? Oh, you think
I'll leave them in the dark about it all?
They shall not know you? Hampden, Pym shall not . . . .

[Enter **PYM, HAMPDEN, VANE**, &c.

[Dropping on his knee.

Thus favoured with your gracious countenance
What shall a rebel League avail against
Your servant, utterly and ever yours?
[To the **REST**]
So, Gentlemen, the King's not even left
The privilege of bidding me farewell
Who haste to save the People—that you style
Your People—from the mercies of the Scots
And France their friend?
[To **CHARLES**]
Pym's grave grey eyes are fixed
Upon you, Sire!
[To the **REST**]
Your pleasure, Gentlemen?

HAMPDEN
The King dissolved us—'tis the King we seek
And not Lord Strafford.

STRAFFORD
. . . . Strafford, guilty too
Of counselling the measure:
[To **CHARLES**]
(Hush . . you know . .
You have forgotten . . Sire, I counselled it!)
—[Aloud] A heinous matter, truly! But the King
Will yet see cause to thank me for a course
Which now, perchance . . (Sire, tell them so!) . . he blames.
Well, choose some fitter time to make your charge—
I shall be with the Scots—you understand?—
Then yelp at me!
Meanwhile, your Majesty
Binds me, by this fresh token of your trust . . .

[Under the pretence of an earnest farewell, **STRAFFORD** conducts **CHARLES** to the door, in such a manner as to hide his agitation from the rest: **VANE** and others gazing at them: as the King disappears, they turn as by one impulse to **PYM**, who has not changed his original posture of surprise.

HAMPDEN
Leave we this arrogant strong wicked man!

VANE and **OTHERS**
Dear Pym! Come out of this unworthy place
To our old room again! Come, dearest Pym!

[**STRAFFORD** just about to follow the King, looks back.

PYM [To **STRAFFORD**]
Keep tryst! the old appointment's made anew:
Forget not we shall meet again!

STRAFFORD
Be it so!
And if an Army follows me?

VANE
His friends
Will entertain your Army!

PYM
I'll not say
You have misreckoned, Strafford: time will . . . .
Perish

Body and spirit! Fool to feign a doubt—
Pretend the scrupulous and nice reserve
Of one whose prowess is to do the feat!
What share have I in it? Shall I affect
To see no dismal sign above your head
When God suspends his ruinous thunder there?
Strafford is doomed!—Touch him no one of you!

[Exeunt **PYM**, **HAMPDEN**, &c.

STRAFFORD
Pym we shall meet again!

[Enter **CARLISLE**.

You here, girl?

CARLISLE
Hush—
I know it all—hush, dearest Strafford!

STRAFFORD
Ah?
Well. I shall make a sorry soldier, Lucy!
All Knights begin their enterprise, you know,
Under the best of auspices; 'tis morn—
The Lady girds his sword upon the Youth—
(He's always very young)—the trumpets sound—
Cups pledge him, and . . . and . . . the King blesses him—
You need not turn a page of the Romance
To learn the Dreadful Giant's fate! Indeed
We've the fair Lady here; but she apart,—
A poor man, never having handled lance,
And rather old, weary, and far from sure
His Squires are not the Giant's friends: well—well—
Let us go forth!

CARLISLE
Go forth?

STRAFFORD
What matters it?
We shall die gloriously—as the book says.

CARLISLE
To Scotland? not to Scotland?
Am I sick
Like your good brother, brave Northumberland?

Beside the walls seem falling on me!

CARLISLE
Strafford,
The wind that saps these walls can undermine
Your camp in Scotland, too! Whence creeps the wind?
Have you no eyes except for Pym? Look here!
A breed of silken creatures lurk and thrive
In your contempt; you'll vanquish Pym? Friend, Vane
Can vanquish you! And Vane you think to fly?—
Rush on the Scots! Do nobly! Vane's slight sneer
Shall test success—adjust the praise—suggest
The faint result: Vane's sneer shall reach you there!
—You do not listen!

STRAFFORD
Oh . . I give that up—
There's fate in it—I give all here quite up.
Care not what Vane does or what Holland does
Against me! 'Tis so idle to withstand them—
In no case tell me what they do!

CARLISLE
But Strafford. . . .

STRAFFORD
I want a little strife, beside—real strife:
This petty, palace-warfare does me harm:
I shall feel better, fairly out of it.

CARLISLE
Why do you smile?

STRAFFORD
I got to fear them, girl!
I could have torn his throat at first, that Vane,
As he leered at me on his stealthy way
To the Queen's closet, Lucy—but of late
I often found it in my heart to say
"Vane—don't traduce me to her!"

CARLISLE
But the King . . .

STRAFFORD
The King stood there, 'tis not so long ago,
—There, and the whisper, Lucy, "Be my friend
Of friends!"—My King! I would have . . .

CARLISLE

. . . Died for him?

STRAFFORD

. . Sworn him true, Lucy: I will die for him.

CARLISLE [Aside]

What can he mean? You'd say he loved him still!
[To **STRAFFORD**]
But go not, Strafford! . . . But you must renounce
This project on the Scots! Die! wherefore die?
Charles never loved you!

STRAFFORD

And he will not, now:
He's not of those who care the more for you
That you're unfortunate.

CARLISLE

Then wherefore die
For such a master?

STRAFFORD

You that told me first
How good he was—when I must leave true friends
To find a truer friend!—that drew me here
From Ireland,—"I had but to show myself
And Charles would spurn Vane, Savile, and the rest"—
You, girl, to ask me that?

CARLISLE [Aside]

If he have set
His heart abidingly on Charles!
[To **STRAFFORD**]
Dear friend
I shall not see you any more!

STRAFFORD

Yes, girl—
There's one man here that I shall meet!

CARLISLE [Aside]

The King!—
What way to save him from the King?
My soul . .
That lent from its own store the charmed disguise
That clothes the King . . he shall behold my soul!

[To **STRAFFORD**]
Strafford . . . (I shall speak best if you'll not gaze
Upon me.) . . . You would perish, too! So sure! . . .
Could you but know what 'tis to bear, my Strafford,
One Image stamped within you, turning blank
The else imperial brilliance of your mind,—
A weakness, but most precious,—like a flaw
I' the diamond which should shape forth some sweet face
Yet to create, and meanwhile treasured there
Lest Nature lose her gracious thought for ever! . . .

STRAFFORD
When could it be? . . . no! . . yet . . was it the day
We waited in the anteroom, till Holland
Should leave the presence-chamber?

CARLISLE
What?

STRAFFORD
—That I
Described to you my love for Charles?

CARLISLE [Aside]
Ah, no—
One must not lure him from a love like that!
Oh, let him love the King and die! 'Tis past. . . .
I shall not serve him worse for that one brief
And passionate hope . . silent for ever now!
[To **STRAFFORD**]
And you are really bound for Scotland, then?
I wish you well: you must be very sure
Of the King's faith, for Pym and all his crew
Will not be idle—setting Vane aside!

STRAFFORD
If Pym is busy,—you may write of Pym.

CARLISLE
What need when there's your king to take your part?
He may endure Vane's counsel; but for Pym—
Think you he'll suffer Pym to . . .

STRAFFORD
Girl, your hair
Is glossier than the Queen's!

CARLISLE

Is that to ask
A curl of me?

STRAFFORD
Scotland—the weary way!

CARLISLE
Stay, let me fasten it.
—A rival's, Strafford?

STRAFFORD [Showing the George]
He hung it there: twine yours around it, girl!

CARLISLE
No—no—another time—I trifle so!
And there's a masque on foot: farewell: the Court
Is dull: do something to enliven us
In Scotland; we expect it at your hands.

STRAFFORD
I shall not fall in Scotland.

CARLISLE
Prosper—if
You'll think of me sometimes!

STRAFFORD
How think of him
And not of you? of you—the lingering streak
(A golden one) in my good fortune's eve?

CARLISLE
Strafford . . . .
Well, when the eve has its last streak
The night has its first star!

[Exit.

STRAFFORD
That voice of hers . . .
You'd think she had a heart sometimes! His voice
Is soft too.
Only God can save him now.
Be Thou about his bed, about his path! . . .
His path! Where's England's path? Diverging wide,
And not to join again the track my foot
Must follow—whither? All that forlorn way—
Among the tombs! Far—far—till . . . What, they do

Then join again, these paths? For, huge in the dusk,
There's—Pym to face!
Why then I have a Foe
To close with, and a fight to fight at last
That's worth my soul! What—do they beard the King—
And shall the King want Strafford at his need—
My King—at his great need? Am I not here?

. . . . Not in the common blessed market-place
Pressed on by the rough artisans, so proud
To catch a glance from Wentworth! They'll lie down
Hungry and say "Why, it must end some day—
Is he not watching for our sake?"
—Not there!
But in Whitehall—the whited sepulchre—
The . . .

[At the Window, and looking on London.

Curse nothing to-night! Only one name
They'll curse in all those streets to-night! Whose fault?
Did I make kings—set up, the first, a man
To represent the multitude, receive
All love in right of them—supplanting them
Until you love the man and not the king—
The man with the mild voice and mournful eyes
That send me forth . . .
To breast the bloody sea
That sweeps before me—with one star to guide—
Night has its first supreme forsaken star!

[Exit.

ACT III

SCENE I.—OPPOSITE WESTMINSTER HALL

SIR HENRY VANE, LORD SAVILE, LORD HOLLAND, and **OTHERS** of the Court.

VANE
The Commons thrust you out?

SAVILE
And what kept you
From sharing their civility?

VANE
Kept me?
Fresh news from Scotland, sir! worse than the last
If that may be! all's up with Strafford there!
Nothing's to bar the mad Scots marching hither
The next fine morning! That detained me, sir!
Well now, before they thrust you out, go on,
Their speaker . . . did the fellow Lenthall say
All we set down for him?

HOLLAND
Not a word missed!
Ere he began, we entered, Savile, I
And Bristol and some more, in hopes to breed
A wholesome awe in the new Parliament—
But such a gang of graceless ruffians, Vane!
They glared at us. . . .

VANE
So many?

SAVILE
Not a bench
Without its complement of burley knaves—
Your son, there, Vane, among them—Hampden leant
Upon his shoulder—think of that!

VANE
I'd think
On Lenthall's speech, if I could get at it . . .
He said, I hope, how grateful they should be
For this unlooked-for summons from the King?

HOLLAND
Just as we drilled him . . .

VANE
That the Scots will march
On London?

HOLLAND
All, and made so much of it
A dozen subsidies at least seemed sure
To follow, when . . .

VANE
Well?

HOLLAND
'Tis a strange thing now!
I've a vague memory of a sort of sound—
A voice—a kind of vast, unnatural voice—
Pym, Sir, was speaking! Savile, help me out,—
What was it all?

SAVILE
Something about "a matter" . . .
No . . "a work for England."

BRISTOL
"England's great revenge"
He talked of.

SAVILE
How should I be used to Pym
More than yourselves?

HOLLAND
However that may be,
'Twas something with which we had nought to do,
For we were "strangers" and 'twas "England's work"—
(All this while looking us straight in the face)
In other words, our presence might be spared:
So, in the twinkling of an eye, before
I settled to my mind what ugly brute
Was likest Pym just then, they yelled us out,
Locked the doors after us, and here are we!

VANE
Old Eliot's method . . .

SAVILE
Ah, now, Vane, a truce
To Eliot and his times, and the great Duke,
And how to manage Parliaments! 'Twas you
Advised the Queen to summon this—why Strafford
To do him justice would not hear of it!

VANE
Say, rather, you have done the best of turns
To Strafford—he's at York—we all know why!
I would you had not set the Scots on Strafford
Till he had put down Pym for us, my lord!

SAVILE
I? did I alter Strafford's plans? did I . . .

[Enter a **MESSENGER**.

MESSENGER
The Queen, my lords . . she sends me . . follow me
At once . . 'tis very urgent . . she would have
Your counsel . . something perilous and strange
Occasions her command.

SAVILE
We follow, friend!
Now Vane . . your Parliament will plague us all!

VANE
No Strafford here beside!

SAVILE
If you dare hint
I had a hand in his betrayal, Sir . . .

HOLLAND
Nay find a fitter time for quarrels—Pym
Will overmatch the best of you; and, think,
The Queen!

VANE
Come on then

[as they go out

. . . understand, I loathe
Strafford as much as any—but he serves
So well to keep off Pym—to screen us all!
I would we had reserved him yet awhile!

[Exeunt.

The **QUEEN** and **CARLISLE**

QUEEN
It cannot be!

CARLISLE
It is so.

QUEEN
Why the House
Have hardly met!

CARLISLE
They met for that.

QUEEN
No—no—
Meet to impeach Lord Strafford! 'Tis a jest!

CARLISLE
A bitter one.

QUEEN
Consider! 'Tis the House
We summoned so reluctantly—which nothing
But the disastrous issue of the war
Persuaded us to summon; they'll wreak all
Their spite on us, no doubt; but the old way
Is to begin by talk of grievances!
They have their grievances to busy them!

CARLISLE
Pym has begun his speech.

QUEEN
Where's Vane? . . That is
Pym will impeach Lord Strafford if he leaves
His Presidency—he's at York, you know,
Since the Scots beat him—why should he leave York?

CARLISLE
Because the King sends for him.

QUEEN
Ah . . . but if
The King did send for him, he let him know
We had been forced to call a Parliament—
A step which Strafford, now I come to think,
Was vehement against . . .

CARLISLE
The policy
Escaped him of first striking Parliaments
To earth, then setting them upon their feet
And giving them a sword: but this is idle!

—Did the King send for Strafford?
He will come.

QUEEN
And what am I to do?

CARLISLE
What do? Fail, Madam!
Be ruined for his sake! what matters how
So it but stand on record that you made
An effort—only one?

QUEEN
The King's away
At Theobald's.

CARLISLE
Send for him at once—he must
Dissolve the House.

QUEEN
Wait till Vane finds the truth
Of the report—then . .

CARLISLE
. . it will matter little
What the king does. Strafford that serves you all—
That's fighting for you now!

[Enter **SIR H. VANE**.

VANE
The Commons, Madam,
Are sitting with closed doors—a huge debate—
No lack of noise—but nothing, I should guess,
Concerning Strafford: Pym has certainly
Not spoken yet.

QUEEN [To **CARLISLE**]
You hear?

CARLISLE
I do not hear
That the King's sent for!

VANE
Savile will be able
To tell you more.

[Enter **HOLLAND**.

QUEEN
The last news, Holland?

HOLLAND
Pym
Is raving like a fiend! The whole House means
To follow him together to Whitehall
And force the King to give up Strafford.

QUEEN
Strafford?

HOLLAND
If they content themselves with Strafford! Laud
Is talked of, Cottington and Windebank too,
Pym has not left out one of them . . I would
You heard Pym raving!

QUEEN
Vane, find out the King!
Tell the king, Vane, the People follow Pym
To brave us at Whitehall!

[Enter **SAVILE**.

SAVILE
Not to Whitehall—
'Tis to the Lords they go—they'll seek redress
On Strafford from his peers—the legal way,
They call it . . .

QUEEN
Wait, Vane!

SAVILE
. . But the adage gives
Long life to threatened men! Strafford can save
Himself so readily: at York, remember,
In his own county, what has he to fear?
The Commons only mean to frighten him
From leaving York.

QUEEN
Surely he will not come!
Carlisle, he will not come!

CARLISLE
Once more, the King
Has sent for Strafford—He will come.

VANE
O doubtless;
And bring destruction with him; that's his way.
What but his coming spoilt all Conway's plan?
The King must take his counsel, choose his friends,
Be wholly ruled by him! What's the result?
The North that was to rise—Ireland to help—
What came of it? In my poor mind a fright
Is no prodigious punishment.

CARLISLE
A fright?
Pym will fail worse than Strafford if he thinks
To frighten him.
[To the **QUEEN**]
You will not save him, then?

SAVILE
When something like a charge is made, the King
Will best know how to save him: and 'tis clear
That, while he suffers nothing by the matter,
The King will reap advantage: this in question,
No dinning you with ship-money complaints!

QUEEN [To **CARLISLE**]
If we dissolve them, who will pay the army?
Protect us from the insolent Scots?

CARLISLE
In truth
I know not, Madam: Strafford's fate concerns
Me little: you desired to learn what course
Would save him: I obey you.

VANE
Notice, too,
There can't be fairer ground for taking full
Revenge—(Strafford's revengeful)—than he'll have
Against this very Pym.

QUEEN
Why, he shall claim
Vengeance on Pym!

VANE
And Strafford, who is he
To 'scape unscathed amid the accidents
That harass all beside? I, for my part,
Should look for something of discomfiture
Had the King trusted me so thoroughly
And been so paid for it.

HOLLAND
He'll keep at York:
All will blow over: he'll return no worse—
Humbled a little—thankful for a place
Under as good a man—Oh, we'll dispense
With seeing Strafford for a month or two!

[Enter **STRAFFORD**.

QUEEN
You here!

STRAFFORD
The King sends for me, Madam.

QUEEN
Sir . . .
The King . . .

STRAFFORD
An urgent matter that imports the King . . .
[To **CARLISLE**]
Why, Lucy, what's in agitation now
That all this muttering and shrugging, see,
Begins at me? They do not speak!

CARLISLE

Oh welcome!
. . And we are proud of you . . . all very proud
To have you with us, Strafford . . you were brave
At Durham . . You did well there . . Had you not
Been stayed you might have . . . . we said, even now,
Our last, last hope's in you!

VANE [To **CARLISLE**]
The Queen would speak
A word with you!

STRAFFORD [To **VANE**]
Will one of you vouchsafe
To signify my presence to the King?

SAVILE
An urgent matter?

STRAFFORD
None that touches you
Lord Savile! Say it were some treacherous,
Sly, pitiful intriguing with the Scots—
You would go free, at least!
[Aside]
They half divine
My purpose!
[To the **QUEEN**]
Madam, shall I see the King?
The service I would render much concerns
His welfare.

QUEEN
But his Majesty, my lord,
May not be here, may . . .

STRAFFORD
Its importance, then,
Must plead excuse for this withdrawal, Madam—
And for the grief it gives Lord Savile here.

QUEEN [Who has been conversing with **VANE** and **HOLLAND**]
The King will see you, Sir.
[To **CARLISLE**]
Mark me: Pym's worst
Is done by now—he has impeached the Earl,
Or found the Earl too strong for him, by now;
Let us not seem instructed! We should work
No good to Strafford, but deform ourselves
With shame in the world's eye!
[To **STRAFFORD**]
His Majesty
Has much to say with you.

STRAFFORD [Aside]
Time fleeting, too!
[To **CARLISLE**]
No means of getting them away, Carlisle?
What does she whisper? Does she know my purpose?
What does she think of it? Get them away!

QUEEN [To **CARLISLE**]
He comes to baffle Pym—he thinks the danger
Far off—tell him no word of it—a time
For help will come—we'll not be wanting, then!
Keep him in play, Carlisle—you, self-possessed
And calm!
[To **STRAFFORD**]
To spare your Lordship some delay
I will myself acquaint the King.
[To **CARLISLE**]
Beware!

[Exeunt **QUEEN**, **VANE**, **HOLLAND** and **SAVILE**.

STRAFFORD
She knows it?

CARLISLE
Tell me, Strafford. . . .

STRAFFORD
Afterward!
The moment's the great moment of all time!
She knows my purpose?

CARLISLE
Thoroughly—just now
She bade me hide it from you.

STRAFFORD
Quick, dear girl . .
The whole grand scheme?

CARLISLE [Aside]
Ah, he would learn if they
Connive at Pym's procedure! Could they but
Have once apprized the King! But there's no time
For falsehood, now.
[To **STRAFFORD**]
Strafford, the whole is known.

STRAFFORD
Known and approved?

CARLISLE
Hardly discountenanced.

STRAFFORD
And the king—say the king consents as well!

CARLISLE
The king's not yet informed, but will not dare
To interpose.

STRAFFORD
What need to wait him, then?
He'll sanction it! I stayed, girl tell him, long!
It vexed me to the soul—this waiting here—
You know him—there's no counting on the king!
Tell him I waited long!

CARLISLE [Aside]
What can he mean?
Rejoice at the king's hollowness?

STRAFFORD
I knew
They would be glad of it,—all over once,
I knew they would be glad . . . but he'd contrive,
The Queen and he, to mar, by helping it,
An angel's making!

CARLISLE [Aside]
Is he mad?
[To **STRAFFORD**]
Dear Strafford,
You were not wont to look so happy.

STRAFFORD
Girl,
I tried obedience thoroughly: I took
The king's wild plan . . . of course, ere I could reach
My army—Conway ruined it: I drew
The wrecks together, raised all heaven and earth,
And would have fought the Scots—the King at once
Made truce with them: then, Lucy, then, dear girl,
God put it my mind to love, serve, die
For Charles—but never to obey him more!
While he endured their insolence at Rippon
I fell on them at Durham!
. . . But you'll tell
The king I waited? All the anteroom
Is filled with my adherents.

CARLISLE

Strafford—Strafford
What daring act is this you hint?

STRAFFORD
No—No!
'Tis here—not daring if you knew!—all here!

[Drawing papers from his breast.

Full proof—see—ample proof—does the Queen know
I have such damning proof? Bedford and Essex,
Broke, Warwick, Savile (did you notice Savile?
The simper that I spoilt?) Say, Mandeville—
Sold to the Scots, body and soul, by Pym!

CARLISLE
Great heaven!

STRAFFORD
From Savile and his lords, to Pym—
I crush them, girl—Pym shall not ward the blow
Nor Savile crawl aside from it! The Court
And the Cabal—I crush them!

CARLISLE
And you go . . .
Strafford,—and now you go? . . .

STRAFFORD
About no work
In the back-ground, I promise you! I go
Straight to the House of Lords to claim these men.
Mainwaring!

CARLISLE
Stay—stay, Strafford!

STRAFFORD
She'll return—
The Queen—some little project of her own—
No time to lose—the King takes fright perhaps—

CARLISLE
Pym's strong, remember!

STRAFFORD
Very strong—as fits
The Faction's Head . . with no offence to Hampden,

Vane, Rudyard and my loving Hollis—one
And all they lodge within the Tower to-night
In just equality. Bryan! Mainwaring!

[Many of his **ADHERENTS** enter.

The Peers debate just now (a lucky chance)
On the Scots war—my visit's opportune:
When all is over, Bryan, you'll proceed
To Ireland: these despatches, mark me, Bryan,
Are for the Deputy, and these for Ormond—
We'll want the Army here—my Army, raised
At such a cost, that should have done such good,
And was inactive all the time! no matter—
We'll find a use for it. Willis . . . no—You!
You, friend, make haste to York—bear this, at once . . .
Or,—better stay for form's sake—see yourself
The news you carry. You remain with me
To execute the Parliament's command,
Mainwaring—help to seize the lesser knaves:
Take care there's no escaping at backdoors!
To not have one escape—mind me—not one!
I seem revengeful, Lucy? Did you know
What these men dare!

CARLISLE
It is so much they dare!

STRAFFORD
I proved that long ago; my turn is now!
Keep sharp watch, Goring, on the citizens;
Observe who harbours any of the brood
That scramble off: be sure they smart for it!
Our coffers are but lean.
And you, girl, too,
Shall have your task—deliver this to Laud—
Laud will not be the slowest in my praise!
"Thorough" he'll say!
—Foolish, to be so glad!
This sort of life is vivid, after all!
'Tis worth while, Lucy, having foes like mine
For the dear bliss of crushing them! To-day
Is worth the living for!

CARLISLE
That reddening brow!
You seem . . .

STRAFFORD

Well—do I not? I would be well—
I could not but be well on such a day!
And, this day ended, 'tis of slight import
How long the ravaged frame subjects the soul
In Strafford!

CARLISLE

Noble Strafford!

STRAFFORD

No farewell!
I'll see you, girl, to-morrow—the first thing!
—If she should come to stay me!

CARLISLE

Go—'tis nothing—
Only my heart that swells—it has been thus
Ere now—go, Strafford!

STRAFFORD

To-night, then, let it be!
I must see Him . . . I'll see you after Him . .
I'll tell you how Pym looked. Follow me, friends!
You, gentlemen, shall see a sight this hour
To talk of all your lives. Close after me!
"My friend of friends!"

[Exeunt **STRAFFORD**, &c.

CARLISLE

The King—ever the King!
No thought of one beside, whose little word
Unveils the King to him—one word from me—
Which yet I do not breathe!
Ah, have I spared
Strafford a pang, and shall I seek reward
Beyond that memory? Surely too, some way
He is the better for my love . . . No, no
He would not look so joyous—I'll believe
His very eye would never sparkle thus,
Had I not prayed for him this long, long while!

[Exit.

SCENE III.—THE ANTECHAMBER OF THE HOUSE OF LORDS

Many of the Presbyterian Party. The Adherents of **STRAFFORD**, &c.

A Group of **PRESBYTERIANS**.

1st PRESBYTERIAN
I tell you he struck Maxwell—Maxwell sought
To stay the Earl: he struck him and passed on.

2nd PRESBYTERIAN
Fear as you may, keep a good countenance
Before these ruffians!

3rd PRESBYTERIAN
Strafford here the first—
With the great army at his back!

4th PRESBYTERIAN
No doubt!
I would Pym had made haste . . . that's Bryan, hush—
The fellow pointing.

STRAFFORD'S Followers.

1st FOLLOWER
Mark these worthies, now!

2nd FOLLOWER
A goodly gathering! "Where the carcass is
There shall the eagles" . . what's the rest?

3rd FOLLOWER
For eagles
Say crows.

A PRESBYTERIAN
Stand back, Sirs!

One of STRAFFORD'S FOLLOWERS
Are we in Geneva?

A PRESBYTERIAN
No—nor in Ireland, we have leave to breathe.

One of STRAFFORD'S FOLLOWERS
Really? Behold how grand a thing it is
To serve "King Pym"! There's some one at Whitehall
That lives obscure, but Pym lives . . .

The PRESBYTERIAN.
Nearer!

A FOLLOWER of STRAFFORD
Higher
We look to see him!
[To his **COMPANIONS**]
I'm to have St. John
In charge; was he among the knaves just now
That followed Pym within there?

ANOTHER
The gaunt man
Talking with Rudyard. Did the Earl expect
Pym at his heels so fast? I like it not.

[Enter **MAXWELL**.

ANOTHER
Why, man, they rush into the net! Here's Maxwell—
Ha, Maxwell?—How the brethren flock around
The fellow! Do you feel the Earl's hand yet
Upon your shoulder, Maxwell?

MAXWELL
Gentlemen,
Stand back! A great thing passes here.

A FOLLOWER of STRAFFORD [To **ANOTHER FOLLOWER**]
The Earl
Is at his work!
[To **MAXWELL**]
Say, Maxwell, what great thing!
Speak out!
[To a **PRESBYTERIAN**]
Friends, I've a kindness for you!
Friends,
I've seen you with St. John . . . O stockishness!
Wear such a ruff, and never call to mind
St. John's head in a charger?
What—the plague—
Not laugh?

ANOTHER
Say Maxwell, what it is!

ANOTHER

Hush—wait—
The jest will be to wait—

1ˢᵗ FOLLOWER
And who's to bear
These quiet hypocrites? You'd swear they came . . .
Came . . . just as we come!

[A **PURITAN** enters hastily and without observing **STRAFFORD'S FOLLOWERS**.

The PURITAN
How goes on the work?
Has Pym . . .

A FOLLOWER of STRAFFORD
The secret's out at last—Aha,
The carrion's scented! Welcome, crow the first!
Gorge merrily you with the blinking eye!
"King Pym has fallen!"

The PURITAN
Pym?

A FOLLOWER of STRAFFORD
Pym!

A PRESBYTERIAN
Only Pym?

Many of STRAFFORD'S FOLLOWERS
No, brother—not Pym only—Vane as well—
Rudyard as well—Hampden—Saint John as well—

A PRESBYTERIAN.
My mind misgives . . can it be true?

ANOTHER
Lost! Lost!

A FOLLOWER of STRAFFORD
Say we true, Maxwell?

The PURITAN.
Pride before destruction,
A haughty spirit goeth before a fall!

Many of STRAFFORD'S FOLOWERS
Ah now! The very thing! A word in season!

A golden apple in a silver picture
To greet Pym as he passes!

[The folding-doors at the back begin to open, noise and light issuing.

MAXWELL
Stand back, all!

Many of the PRESBYTERIANS.
I'll die with Pym! And I!

STRAFFORD'S FOLLOWERS
Now for the text—
He comes! Quick!

The PURITAN [With uplifted arms]
How hath the Oppressor ceased!
The Lord hath broken the staff of the wicked:
The sceptre of the Rulers—he who smote
The People in wrath with a continual stroke—
That ruled the nations in his anger . . . He
Is persecuted and none hindereth!

[At the beginning of this speech, the doors open, and **STRAFFORD** in the greatest disorder, and amid cries from within of "Void the House," staggers out. When he reaches the front of the Stage, silence.

STRAFFORD
Impeach me! Pym! I never struck, I think,
The felon on that calm insulting mouth
When it proclaimed—Pym's mouth proclaimed me . .
God!
Was it a word, only a word that held
The outrageous blood back on my heart . . which beats!
Which beats! Some one word . . . "Traitor," did he say
Bending that eye, brimful of bitter fire,
Upon me?

MAXWELL [Advancing]
In the Commons' name, their servant
Demands Lord Strafford's sword.

STRAFFORD
What did you say?

MAXWELL
The Commons bid me ask your Lordship's sword.

STRAFFORD [suddenly recovering, and looking round, draws it, and turns to his followers]

Let us go forth—follow me, gentlemen—
Draw your swords too—cut any down that bar us!
On the King's service! Maxwell, clear the way!

[The **PRESBYTERIANS** prepare to dispute his passage.

STRAFFORD
Ha—true! . . . That is, you mistake me, utterly—
I will stay—the King himself shall see me—here—
Here—I will stay, Mainwaring!—First of all,
[To **MAXWELL**]
Your tablets, fellow!

[He writes on them]

[To **MAINWARING**]
Give that to the King!
Yes, Maxwell, for the next half-hour, I will . . .
I will remain your prisoner, I will!
Nay, you shall take my sword!

[**MAXWELL** advances to take it.

No—no—not that!
Their blood, perhaps, may wipe out all thus far—
All up to that—not that! Why, friend, you see
When the King lays his head beneath my foot
It will not pay for that! Go, all of you!

MAXWELL
I grieve, my lord, to disobey: none stir.

STRAFFORD
This gentle Maxwell!—Do not touch him, Bryan!
[To the **PRESBYTERIAN**]
Whichever cur of you will carry this
I'll save him from the fate of all the rest—
I'll have him made a Peer—I'll . . . none will go?
None?

[Cries from within of "STRAFFORD".

[To his **FOLLOWERS**]
Slingsby, I've loved you at least—my friend,
Stab me! I have not time to tell you why . . .
You then, dear Bryan! You Mainwaring, then!
. . . Ah, that's because I spoke so hastily
At Allerton—the King had vexed me . . .

[To the **PRESBYTERIANS**]
You
Miscreants—you then—that I'll exterminate!
—Not even you? If I live over it
The King is sure to have your heads—you know
I'm not afraid of that—you understand
That if I chose to wait—made up my mind
To live this minute—he would do me right!
But what if I can't live this minute through?
If nothing can repay that minute? Pym
With his pursuing smile—Pym to be there!

[Louder cries of "STRAFFORD".

The King! I troubled him—stood in the way
Of his negotiations—was the one
Great obstacle to peace—the Enemy
Of Scotland—and he sent for me—from York—
My safety guaranteed—having prepared
A Parliament! I see! And at Whitehall
The Queen was whispering with Vane . . . I see
The trap! I curse the King! I wish Pym well!
Wish all his brave friends well! Say, all along
Strafford was with them—all along, at heart,
I hated Charles and wished them well! And say

[Tearing off the George and dashing it down.

That as I tread this gew-gaw under foot,
I cast his memory from me! One stroke, now!

[His own **ADHERENTS** disarm him. Renewed cries of "STRAFFORD".

I'll not go . . . they shall drag me by the hair!

[Changing suddenly to calm.

England! I see her arm in this! I yield.
Why—'tis the fairest triumph! Why desire
To cheat them? I would never stoop to that—
Be mean enough for that! Let all have end!
Don't repine, Slingsby . . .have they not a right?
They claim me—hearken—lead me to them, Bryan!
No—I myself should offer up myself.
Pray you now . . . Pym awaits me . . . pray you now!

[Putting aside those who attempt to support him, **STRAFFORD** reaches the doors—they open wide.
HAMPDEN, &c. and a crowd discovered; and at the bar, **PYM** standing apart. As **STRAFFORD** kneels

the scene shuts.

SCENE I.—WHITEHALL

The **KING**, the **QUEEN**, **HOLLIS**, **CARLISLE**. **VANE**, **HOLLAND**, **SAVILE**, in the back-ground.

CARLISLE
Answer them, Hollis, for his sake!—One word!

CHARLES [To **HOLLIS**]
You stand, silent and cold, as though I were
Deceiving you—my friend, my playfellow
Of other times! What wonder after all?
Just so I dreamed my People loved me!

HOLLIS
Sire,
It is yourself that you deceive, not me!
You'll quit me comforted—your mind made up
That since you've talked thus much and grieved thus much,
All you can do for Strafford has been done.

QUEEN
If you kill Strafford . . . come, we grant you leave,
Suppose . . .

HOLLIS
I may withdraw, Sire?

CARLISLE
Hear them out!
'Tis the last chance for Strafford! Hear them out!

HOLLIS
"If we kill Strafford"—on the eighteenth day
Of Strafford's trial—We!

CHARLES
Pym, my good Hollis—
Pym, I should say!

HOLLIS
Ah, true—Sire, pardon me!
You witness our proceedings every day,

But the screened gallery, I might have guessed,
Admits of such a partial glimpse at us—
Pym takes up all the room, shuts out the view!
Still, on my honour, Sire, the rest of the place
Is not unoccupied: the Commons sit
—That's England; Ireland sends, and Scotland too,
Their representatives: the Peers that judge
Are easily distinguished; one remarks
The People here and there . . . but the close curtain
Must hide so much!

QUEEN
Acquaint your insolent crew,
This day the curtain shall be dashed aside!
It served a purpose!

HOLLIS
Think! This very day?
Ere Strafford rises to defend himself?

CHARLES
I will defend him, Sir! sanction the past—
This day—it ever was my purpose! Rage
At me, not Strafford! Oh I shall be paid
By Strafford's look!

CARLISLE [To **HOLLIS**]
Nobly! Oh will he not
Do nobly?

HOLLIS
Sire, you will do honestly;
And, for that look, I too would be a king!

CHARLES [after a pause]
Only, to do this now—just when they seek
To make me out a tyrant—one that's deaf
To subjects' prayers,—shall I oppose them now?
It seems their will the Trial should proceed . . .
'Tis palpably their will!

HOLLIS
You'll lose your throne:
But it were no bright moment save for that!
Strafford, your prime support, the sole roof-tree
That props this quaking House of Privilege,
(Floods come, winds beat, and see—the treacherous sand!)
Doubtless if the mere putting forth an arm

Could save him, you'd save Strafford!

CHARLES
And they mean
Calmly to consummate this wrong! No hope?
This ineffaceable wrong! No pity then?

HOLLIS
No plague in store for perfidy?—Farewell!
You summoned me . . .
[To **CARLISLE**]
You, Lady, bade me come
To save the Earl! I came, thank God for it,
To learn how far such perfidy can go!
. . . You dare to talk with me of saving him
Who have just ruined Strafford!

CHARLES
I?

HOLLIS
See, now!
Eighteen days long he throws, one after one,
Our charges back: a blind moth-eaten law!
—He'll break from us at last! And whom to thank?
The Mouse that gnawed the Lion's net for him
Got a good friend,—but he, the other Mouse,
That looked on while the Lion freed himself—
Fared he so well, does any fable say?

CHARLES
What can you mean?

HOLLIS
Pym never could have proved
Strafford's design of bringing up the troops
To force this kingdom to obedience: Vane—
Your servant, Vane . . .

QUEEN
Well, Sir?

HOLLIS
. . Has proved it.

CHARLES
Vane?

HOLLIS

This day! Did Vane deliver up or no
Those notes which, furnished by his son to Pym,
Have sealed . . .

CHARLES

Speak Vane! As I shall live, I know
Nothing that Vane has done! What treason next?
I wash my hands of it! Vane, speak the truth!
—Ask Vane himself!

HOLLIS

I will not speak to Vane
Who speak to Pym and Hampden every day!

QUEEN

Speak to Vane's master then! Why should he wish
For Strafford's death?

HOLLIS

Why? Strafford cannot turn
As you sit there—bid you come forth and say
If every hateful act were not set down
In his commission?—Whether you contrived
Or no that all the violence should seem
His work, the gentle ways—your own, as if
He counteracted your kind impulses
While . . . but you know what he could say! And then
Would he produce, mark you, a certain charge
To set your own express commands aside,
If need were, and be blameless! He'd say, then . . . .

CHARLES

Hold!

HOLLIS

. . . . Say who bade him break the Parliament,—
Find out some pretext to set up sword-law . . .

QUEEN

Retire, Sir!

CHARLES

Vane—once more—what Vane dares do
I know not . . . he is rash . . . a fool . . . I know
Nothing of Vane!

HOLLIS

Well—I believe you; Sire
Believe me, in return, that . . .
[Turning to **CARLISLE**]
Gentle Lady,
The few words I would say the stones might hear
Sooner than these . . . I'll say them all to you,
You, with the heart! The question, trust me, takes
Another shape, to-day: 'tis not if Charles
Or England shall succumb,—but which shall pay
The forfeit, Strafford or his Master: Sire,
You loved me once . . . think on my warning now!

[Exit.

CHARLES
On you and on your warning both!—Carlisle!
That paper!

QUEEN
But consider!

CHARLES
Give it me!
There—signed—will that content you?—Do not speak!
You have betrayed me, Vane!—See—any day
(According to the tenour of that paper)
He bids your brother bring the Army up,
Strafford shall head it and take full revenge!
Seek Strafford! Let him have it, look, before
He rises to defend himself!

QUEEN
In truth?
Clever of Hollis, now, to work a change
Like this! You were reluctant . . .

CHARLES
Say, Carlisle
Your brother Percy brings the Army up—
Falls on the Parliament—(I'll think of you
My Hollis!)—say we plotted long . . . 'tis mine,
The scheme is mine, remember! Say I cursed
Vane's folly in your hearing! If that man
Does rise to do us shame, the fault shall lie
With you, Carlisle!

CARLISLE
Nay, fear not me! but still

That's a bright moment, Sire, you throw away . . .
Oh, draw the veil and save him!

QUEEN
Go, Carlisle!

CARLISLE [aside, and going]
I shall see Strafford—speak to him: my heart
Must never beat so, then!
And if I tell
The truth? What's gained by falsehood? There they stand
Whose trade it is—whose life it is! How vain
To gild such rottenness! Strafford shall know,
Thoroughly know them!

THE QUEEN [As she leaves the **KING**, &c.]
Trust to me!
[To **CARLISLE**]
Carlisle,
You seem inclined, alone of all the Court,
To serve poor Strafford: this bold plan of yours
Merits much praise, and yet . . .

CARLISLE
Time presses, Madam.

QUEEN
Yet . . . may it not be something premature?
Strafford defends himself to-day—reserves
Some wondrous effort . . one may well suppose—
He'll say some overwhelming fact, Carlisle!

CARLISLE
Aye, Hollis hints as much.

CHARLES
Why linger then?
Haste with the scheme—my scheme—I shall be there
To watch his look! Tell him I watch his look!

QUEEN
Stay, we'll precede you!

CARLISLE
At your pleasure.

CHARLES
Say . . .

Say . . Vane is hardly ever at Whitehall!
I shall be there, remember!

CARLISLE
Doubt me not!

CHARLES
On our return, Carlisle, we wait you here!

CARLISLE
I'll bring his answer; Sire, I follow you.

[Exeunt **KING** &c.

Ah . . . but he would be very sad to find
The King so faithless, and I take away
All that he cares to live for: let it go—
'Tis the King's scheme!
My Strafford, I can save . . .
Nay, I have saved you—yet am scarce content,
Because my poor name will not cross your mind . . .
Strafford, how much I am unworthy you!

[Exit.

SCENE II.—A PASSAGE ADJOINING WESTMINSTER HALL

Many groups of **SPECTATORS** of the Trial (which is visible from the back of the Stage)—**OFFICERS** of the
Court, &c.

FIRST SPECTATOR
More crowd than ever! . . . Not know Hampden, man?
That's he—by Pym—Pym that is speaking now!
No, truly—if you look so high you'll see
Little enough of either!

SECOND SPECTATOR
Hush . . . Pym's arm
Points like a prophet's rod!

THIRD SPECTATOR
Ay—ay—we've heard
Some pretty speaking . . yet the Earl escapes!

FOURTH SPECTATOR
I fear it: just a foolish word or two

About his children . . . and they see, forsooth,
Not England's Foe in Strafford—but the Man
Who, sick, half-blind . . .

SECOND SPECTATOR
What's that Pym's saying now
That makes the curtains flutter . . look! A hand
Clutches them . . Ah! The King's hand!

FIFTH SPECTATOR
I had thought
Pym was not near so tall! What said he, friend?

SECOND SPECTATOR
"Nor is this way a novel way of blood" . . .
And the Earl turns as if to . . . look! look!

MANY SPECTATORS
Heaven—
What ails him . . no—he rallies . . see—goes on
And Strafford smiles. Strange!

[Enter a **PURITAN**.

THE PURITAN
Haselrig.

MANY SPECTATORS
Friend? Friend?

THE PURITAN
Lost—utterly lost . . just when we looked for Pym
To make a stand against the ill effects
Of the Earl's speech! Is Haselrig without?
Pym's message is to him!

[Exit.

THIRD SPECTATOR
Now, said I true?
Will the Earl leave them yet at fault or no?

FIRST SPECTATOR
Never believe it, man! These notes of Vane's
Ruin the Earl!

FIFTH SPECTATOR
A brave end . . not a whit

Less firm, less . . . Pym all over! Then the Trial
Is closed . . . no . . .Strafford means to speak again!

AN OFFICER
Stand back, there!

FIFTH SPECTATOR
Why the Earl is coming hither!
Before the court breaks up! His brother, look,—
You'd say he deprecated some fierce act
In Strafford's mind just now!

AN OFFICER
Stand back, I say!

SECOND SPECTATOR
Who's the veiled woman that he talks with?

MANY SPECTATORS
Hush—
The Earl! the Earl!

[Enter **STRAFFORD**, **SLINGSBY** and other **SECRETARIES**, **HOLLIS**, **CARLISLE**, **MAXWELL**, **BALFOUR**, &c.
STRAFFORD converses with **CARLISLE**.

HOLLIS
So near the end! Be patient—
Return!

STRAFFORD [To his **SECRETARIES**]
Here—anywhere—or—'tis freshest here . .
(To spend one's April here—the blossom-month!)
Set it down here!

[They arrange a table, papers &c.

What, Pym to quail, to sink
Because I glance at him, yet . . .
Well, to end—
What's to be answered, Slingsby? Let us end!
[To **CARLISLE**]
Girl, I refuse his offer; whatsoe'er
It be! Too late! Tell me no word of him!
[To **HOLLIS**]
'Tis something, Hollis, I assure you that—
To stand, sick as you are, some eighteen days
Fighting for life and fame against a pack
Of very curs, that lie thro' thick and thin,

Eat flesh and bread by wholesale, and can't say
"Strafford" if it would take my life!

CARLISLE
Be kind
This once! Glance at the paper . . if you will
But glance at it . . .

STRAFFORD
Already at my heels!
Pym's faulting bloodhounds scent the track again!
Peace, girl! Now, Slingsby!

[**MESSENGERS** from Lane and other of **STRAFFORD'S** Counsel within the Hall are coming and going during the Scene.

STRAFFORD [Setting himself to write and dictate]
I shall beat you, Hollis!
Do you know that? In spite of all your tricks—
In spite of Pym! Your Pym that shrank from me!
Eliot would have contrived it otherwise!
[To a **MESSENGER**]
In truth? This slip, tell Lane, contains as much
As I can call to mind about the matter.
[To **HOLLIS**]
Eliot would have disdained . . .
[Calling after the **MESSENGER**]
And Radcliffe, say—
The only person who could answer Pym—
Is safe in prison, just for that!
[Continuing to **HOLLIS**]
Well—well—
It had not been recorded in that case,
I baffled you!
[To **CARLISLE**]
Nay, girl, why look so grieved?
All's gained without the King! You saw Pym quail?
. . . What shall I do when they acquit me, think you,
But tranquilly resume my task as though
Nothing had intervened since I proposed
To call that traitor to account! Such tricks,
Trust me, shall not be played a second time—
Even against old Laud, with his grey hair . . .
Your good work, Hollis!—And to make amends
You, Lucy, shall be there when I impeach
Pym and his fellows!

HOLLIS

Wherefore not protest
Against our whole proceeding long ago?
Why feel indignant now? Why stand this while
Enduring patiently . . .

STRAFFORD [To **CARLISLE**]
Girl, I'll tell you—
You—and not Pym . . you, the slight graceful girl
Tall for a flowering lily—and not Charles . . .
Why I stood patient! I was fool enough
To see the will of England in Pym's will—
To dream that I had wronged her—and to wait
Her judgment,—when, behold, in place of it . . .
[To a **MESSENGER** who whispers]
Tell Lane to answer no such question! Law . . .
I grapple with their Law! I'm here to try
My actions by their standard, not my own!
Their Law allowed that levy . . . what's the rest
To Pym, or Lane, or any but myself?

CARLISLE
Then cast not thus your only chance away—
The King's so weak . . secure this chance! 'Twas Vane
—Vane, recollect, who furnished Pym the notes . . .

STRAFFORD
Fit . . very fit . . those precious notes of Vane,
To close the Trial worthily! I feared
Some spice of nobleness might linger yet
To spoil the character of all the past!
It pleased me . . and (rising passionately) I will go back and say
As much—to them—to England! Follow me!
I have a word to say! There! my defence
Is done!
[To **CARLISLE**]
Stay . . why be proud? Why care to own
My gladness—my surprise? . . no—not surprise!
Oh, why insist upon the little pride
Of doing all myself and sparing him
The pain? Girl, say the triumph is my King's!
When Pym grew pale, and trembled, and sank down—
His image was before me . . . could I fail?
Girl, care not for the past—so indistinct—
Obscure—there's nothing to forgive in it
'Tis so forgotten! From this day begins
A new life, founded on a new belief
In Charles . . .

HOLLIS

Pym comes . . tell Pym it is unfair!
Appeal to Pym! Hampden—and Vane! see, Strafford!
Say how unfair . . .

STRAFFORD

To Pym? I would say nothing!
I would not look upon Pym's face again!

CARLISLE

Stay . . let me have to think I pressed your hand!

[Exeunt **STRAFFORD** &c.

[Enter **HAMPDEN** and **VANE.**

VANE

O Hampden, save that great misguided man!
Plead Strafford's cause with Pym—I have remarked
He moved no muscle when we all spoke loud
Against him . . . you had but to breathe—he turned
Those kind, large eyes upon you—kind to all
But Strafford . . whom I murder!

[Enter **PYM**, conversing with the Solicitor-General, **St. JOHN**, the Managers of the Trial, **FIENNES**, **RUDYARD**, &c.)

RUDYARD

Horrible!
Till now all hearts were with you . . . I withdraw
For one! Too horrible! Oh we mistake
Your purpose, Pym . . you cannot snatch away
The last spar from the drowning man!

FIENNES

He talks
With St. John of it—see how quietly!
[To other **PRESBYTERIANS**]
You'll join us? Mind, we own he merits death—
But this new course is monstrous! Vane, take heart!
This Bill of his Attainder shall not have
One true man's hand to it!

VANE

But hear me, Pym!
Confront your Bill—your own Bill . . what is it?
You cannot catch the Earl on any charge . .
No man will say the Law has hold of him

On any charge . . and therefore you resolve
To take the general sense on his desert,—
As though no Law existed, and we met
To found one!—You refer to every man
To speak his thought upon this hideous mass
Of half-borne out assertions—dubious hints
Hereafter to be cleared—distortions—aye,
And wild inventions. Every man is saved
The task of fixing any single charge
On Strafford: he has but to see in him
The Enemy of England . . .

PYM
A right scruple!
I have heard some called England's Enemy
With less consideration.

VANE
Pity me!
Me—brought so low—who hoped to do so much
For England—her true servant—Pym, your friend . . .
Indeed you made me think I was your friend!
But I have murdered Strafford . . I have been
The instrument of this! who shall remove
That memory from me?

PYM
I absolve you, Vane!
Take you no care for aught that you have done!

VANE
Dear Hampden, not this Bill! Reject this Bill!
He staggers thro' the ordeal . . . let him go!
Strew no fresh fire before him! Plead for us
With Pym . . what God is he, to have no heart
Like ours, yet make us love him?

RUDYARD
Hampden, plead
For us! When Strafford spoke your eyes were thick
With tears . . save him, dear Hampden!

HAMPDEN
England speaks
Louder than Strafford! Who are we, to play
The generous pardoner at her expense—
Magnanimously waive advantages—
And if he conquer us. . . . applaud his skill?

VANE [To **PYM**]
He was your friend!

PYM
I have heard that before.

FIENNES
But England trusts you . . .

HAMPDEN
Shame be his, who turns
The opportunity of serving her
She trusts him with, to his own mean account—
Who would look nobly frank at her expense!

FIENNES
I never thought it could have come to this!

PYM [turning from **St. JOHN**]
But I have made myself familiar, Fiennes,
With that one thought—have walked, and sat, and slept,
That thought before me! I have done such things,
Being the chosen man that should destroy
This Strafford! You have taken up that thought
To play with—for a gentle stimulant—
To give a dignity to idler life
By the dim prospect of this deed to come . . .
But ever with the softening, sure belief,
That all would come some strange way right at last!

FIENNES
Had we made out some weightier charge . . . .

PYM
You say
That these are petty charges! Can we come
To the real charge at all? There he is safe!
In tyranny's strong hold! Apostasy
Is not a crime—Treachery not a crime!
The cheek burns, the blood tingles, when you name
Their names, but where's the power to take revenge
Upon them? We must make occasion serve:
The Oversight, pay for the Giant Sin
That mocks us!

RUDYARD
But this unexampled course—

This Bill. . . .

PYM
By this, we roll the clouds away
Of Precedent and Custom, and at once
Bid the great light which God has set in all,
The conscience of each bosom, shine upon
The guilt of Strafford: each shall lay his hand
Upon his breast, and say if this one man
Deserve to die, or no, by those he sought
First to undo.

FIENNES
You, Vane—you answer him!

VANE
Pym, you see farthest . . . I can only see
Strafford . . . I'd not pass over that pale corse
For all beyond!

RUDYARD and **OTHERS**.
Pym, you would look so great!
Forgive him! He would join us! now he finds
How false the King has been! The pardon, too,
Should be your own! Yourself should bear to Strafford
The pardon of the Commons!

PYM [starting]
Meet him? Strafford?
Have we to meet once more, then? Be it so!
And yet—the prophecy seemed half fulfilled
When, at the trial, as he gazed—my youth—
Our friendship—all old thoughts came back at once
And left me, for a time . . . .

VANE [aside to **RUDYARD**]
Moved, is he not?

PYM
To-morrow we discuss the points of law
With Lane . . .to-morrow!

VANE
Time enough, dear Pym!
See, he relents! I knew he would relent!

PYM
The next day, Haselrig, you introduce,

The Bill of his Attainder.

[After a pause.

Pray for me!

SCENE III.—WHITEHALL

The **KING**.

CHARLES
Strafford, you are a Prince! Not to reward you
—Nothing does that—but only for a whim!
My noble servant!—To defend himself
Thus irresistibly . . withholding aught
That seemed to implicate us!
We have done
Less gallantly by Strafford! Well, the future
Must recompense the past.
She tarries long!
I understand you, Strafford, now!
The scheme—
Carlisle's mad scheme—he'll sanction it, I fear,
For love of me! 'Twas too precipitate:
Before the Army's fairly on its march,
He'll be at large: no matter . .
Well, Carlisle?

[Enter **PYM**.

PYM
Fear me not, Sire . . . my mission is to save,
This time!

CHARLES
To break thus on me!—Unannounced . . .

PYM
It is of Strafford I would speak.

CHARLES
No more
Of Strafford! I have heard too much from you!

PYM
I spoke, Sire, for the People: will you hear

A word upon my own account?

CHARLES
Of Strafford?
[Aside]
So, turns the tide already? Have we tamed
The insolent brawler?—Strafford's brave defence
Is swift in its effect!
[To **PYM**]
Lord Strafford, Sir,
Has spoken for himself!

PYM
Sufficiently.
I would apprize you of the novel course
The people take: the Trial fails, . . .

CHARLES
Yes—yes—
We are aware, Sir: for your part in it
Means shall be found to thank you.

PYM
Pray you, read
This schedule!

[As the **KING** reads it.

I would learn from your own mouth
—(It is a matter much concerning me)—
Whether, if two Estates of England shall concede
The death of Strafford, on the grounds set forth
Within that parchment, you, Sire, can resolve
To grant your full consent to it. That Bill
Is framed by me: if you determine, Sire,
That England's manifested will shall guide
Your judgment, ere another week that will
Shall manifest itself. If not,—I cast
Aside the measure.

CHARLES
. . You can hinder, then,
The introduction of that Bill?

PYM
I can.

CHARLES

He is my friend, Sir: I have wronged him: mark you,
Had I not wronged him—this might be!—You think
Because you hate the Earl . . . (turn not away—
We know you hate him)—no one else could love
Strafford . . . but he has saved me—many times—
Think what he has endured . . proud too . . you feel
What he endured!—And, do you know one strange,
One frightful thing? We all have used that man
As though he had been ours . . with not a source
Of happy thoughts except in us . . and yet
Strafford has children, and a home as well,
Just as if we had never been! . . Ah Sir,
You are moved—you—a solitary man
Wed to your cause—to England if you will!

PYM
Yes . . .think, my soul . . .to England! Draw not back!

CHARLES
Prevent that Bill, Sir . . .Oh, your course was fair
Till now! Why, in the end, 'tis I should sign
The warrant for his death! You have said much
That I shall ponder on; I never meant
Strafford should serve me any more: I take
The Commons' counsel: but this Bill is yours—
Not worthy of its leader . . .care not, Sir,
For that, however! I will quite forget
You named it to me! You are satisfied?

PYM
Listen to me, Sire! Eliot laid his hand,
Wasted and white, upon my forehead once;
Wentworth . . . he's gone now! . . has talked on, whole nights,
And I beside him; Hampden loves me; Sire,
How can I breathe and not wish England well—
And her King well?

CHARLES
I thank you, Sir! You leave
That King his servant! Thanks, Sir!

PYM
Let me speak
—Who may not speak again! whose spirit yearns
For a cool night after this weary day!
—Who would not have my heart turn sicker yet
In a new task, more fatal, more august
More full of England's utter weal or woe . . .

I thought, Sire, could I find myself with you—
After this Trial—alone—as man to man—
I might say something—warn you—pray you—save you—
Mark me, King Charles, save—you!
But God must do it. Yet I warn you, Sire—
(With Strafford's faded eyes yet full on me)
As you would have no deeper question moved
—"How long the Many shall endure the One" . . .
Assure me, Sire, if England shall assent
To Strafford's death, you will not interfere!
Or—

CHARLES
God forsakes me—I am in a net . . .
I cannot move! Let all be as you say!

[Enter **CARLISLE.**

CARLISLE
He loves you—looking beautiful with joy
Because you sent me! he would spare you all
The pain! he never dreamed you would forsake
Your servant in the evil day—nay, see
Your scheme returned! That generous heart of his!
He needs it not—or, needing it, disdains
A course that might endanger you—you, Sire,
Whom Strafford from his inmost soul . . .
[Seeing **PYM**]
No fear—
No fear for Strafford! all that's true and brave
On your own side shall help us! we are now
Stronger than ever!
Ha—what, Sire, is this?
All is not well! What parchment have you there?

[**CHARLES** drops it, and exit.

PYM
Sire, much is saved us both: farewell!

CARLISLE
Stay—stay—
This cursed measure—you'll not dare—you mean
To frighten Charles! This Bill—look—

[As **PYM** reads it.

Why, your lip

Whitens—you could not read one line to me
Your voice would falter so! It shakes you now—
And will you dare . . .

PYM
No recreant yet to her!
The great word went from England to my soul,
And I arose! The end is very near!

[Exit.

CARLISLE
I save him! All have shrunk from him beside—
'Tis only I am left! Heaven will make strong
The hand as the true heart! Then let me die!

[Exit.

ACT V

SCENE I.—WHITEHALL

HOLLIS, CARLISLE

HOLLIS
Tell the King, then! Come in with me!

CARLISLE
Not so!
He must not hear 'till it succeeds!

HOLLIS
Vain! Vain!
No dream was half so vain—you'll rescue Strafford
And outwit Pym! I cannot tell you . . . girl,
The block pursues me—all the hideous show . . .
To-day . . . is it to-day? And all the while
He's sure of the King's pardon . . .think, I have
To tell this man he is to die!
The King
May rend his hair, for me! I'll not see Strafford!

CARLISLE
Only, if I succeed, remember—Charles
Has saved him! He would hardly value life
Unless his gift.

My staunch friends wait! Go in—
You must go in to Charles!

HOLLIS
And all beside
Left Strafford long ago—the King has signed
The warrant for his death . . .the Queen was sick
Of the eternal subject! For the Court,—
The Trial was amusing in its way
Only too much of it . . .the Earl withdrew
In time! But you—fragile—alone—so young!
Amid rude mercenaries—you devised
A plan to save him! Even tho' it fails
What shall reward you?

CARLISLE
I may go, you think,
To France with him? And you reward me, friend!
Who lived with Strafford even from his youth
Before he set his heart on state-affairs
And they bent down that noble brow of his—
I have learned somewhat of his latter life
And all the future I shall know—but, Hollis,
I ought to make his youth my own as well!
Tell me—when he is saved!

HOLLIS
My gentle girl
He should know all—should love you—but 'tis vain!

CARLISLE
No—no—too late now! Let him love the King!
'Tis the King's scheme! I have your word—remember!—
We'll keep the old delusion up! But, hush!
Hush! Each of us has work to do, beside!
Go to the King! I hope—Hollis—I hope!
Say nothing of my scheme! Hush, while we speak
Think where He is! Now for my gallant friends!

[Exit.

HOLLIS
Where He is! Calling wildly upon Charles—
Guessing his fate—pacing the prison-floor . . .
Let the King tell him! I'll not look on Strafford!

[Exit.

STRAFFORD sitting with his **CHILDREN**. They sing.

O bell' andare
Per barca in mare,
Verso la sera
Di Primavera!

WILLIAM
(The boat's in the broad moonlight all this while)

Verso la sera
Di Primavera.

And the boat shoots from underneath the moon
Into the shadowy distance—only still
You hear the dipping oar,

Verso la sera . . .

And faint—and fainter—and then all's quite gone,
Music and light and all, like a lost star.

ANNE
But you should sleep, father: you were to sleep!

STRAFFORD
I do sleep, dearest; or if not—you know
There's such a thing as . . .

WILLIAM
You're too tired to sleep?

STRAFFORD
It will come by and bye and all day long,
In that old quiet house I told you of:
We'll sleep safe there.

ANNE
Why not in Ireland?

STRAFFORD
Ah!
Too many dreams!—That song's for Venice, William:
You know how Venice looks upon the map . . .

Isles that the mainland hardly can let go?

WILLIAM
You've been to Venice, father?

STRAFFORD
I was young then.

WILLIAM
A city with no King; that's why I like
Even a song that comes from Venice!

STRAFFORD
William!

WILLIAM
Oh, I know why! Anne, do you love the King?
But I'll see Venice for myself one day.

STRAFFORD
See many lands, boy—England last of all,—
That way you'll love her best.

WILLIAM
Why do men say
You sought to ruin her, then!

STRAFFORD
Ah . . . they say that.

WILLIAM
Why?

STRAFFORD
I suppose they must have words to say.
As you to sing.

ANNE
But they make songs beside:
Last night I heard one, in the street beneath,
That named you . . . Oh, the names!

WILLIAM
Don't mind her, father!
They soon left off when I called out to them!

STRAFFORD
We shall so soon be out of it, my boy!

'Tis not worth while: who heeds a foolish song?

WILLIAM
Why, not the King!

STRAFFORD
Well: it has been the fate
Of better men, and yet. . . . why not feel sure
That Time, who in the twilight comes to mend
All the fantastic Day's caprice—consign
Unto the ground once more the ignoble Term,
And raise the Genius on his orb again—
That Time will do me right?

ANNE
Shall we sing, William?
He does not look thus when we sing.

STRAFFORD
For Ireland,—
Something is done . . .too little, but enough
To show what might have been:—

WILLIAM
I have no heart
To sing now! Anne, how very sad he looks!
Oh I so hate the King for all he says!

STRAFFORD
Forsook them! What, the common songs will run
That I forsook the People? Nothing more?
. . . Aye, Fame, the scribe, will pause awhile, no doubt,
Turning a deaf ear to her thousand slaves
Noisy to be enrolled,—will register
All curious glosses, subtle notices,
Ingenious clearings-up one fain would see
Beside that plain inscription of The Name—
The Patriot Pym, or the Apostate Strafford!

[The **CHILDREN** resume their song timidly, but break off.

[Enter **HOLLIS** and an **ATTENDANT**.

STRAFFORD
No . . . Hollis? in good time!—Who is he?

HOLLIS
One

That must be present.

STRAFFORD
Ah—I understand—
They will not let me see poor Laud alone!
How politic! They'd use me by degrees
To solitude: and just as you came in
I was solicitous what life to lead
When Strafford's "not so much as Constable
In the King's service." Is there any means
To keep one's self awake? What would you do
After this bustle, Hollis, in my place?

HOLLIS
Strafford . . .

STRAFFORD
Observe, not but that Pym and you
Will find me news enough—news I shall hear
Under a quince tree by a fish-pond side
At Wentworth. Or, a better project now—
What if when all is over, and the Saints
Reign, and the Senate goes on swimmingly,—
What if I venture up, some day, unseen—
To saunter through the Town—notice how Pym,
The Tribune, likes Whitehall—drop quietly
Into a tavern—hear a point discussed—
As, whether Strafford's name were John or Richard—
And be myself appealed to . . . I, who shall
Myself have near forgotten!

HOLLIS
I would speak . . .

STRAFFORD
Then you shall speak,—not now: I want, just now,
To hear the sound of my own tongue. This place
Is full of ghosts!

HOLLIS
Will you not hear me, Strafford?

STRAFFORD
Oh, readily! . . . Only, one droll thing more,—
The minister! Who will advise the King,
And yet have health—children, for aught I know!
—My patient pair of traitors! Ah . . .but, William—
Does not his cheek grow thin?

WILLIAM
'Tis you look thin,
Father!

STRAFFORD
A scamper o'er the breezy wolds
Sets all to-rights!

HOLLIS
You cannot sure forget
A prison-roof is o'er you, Strafford?

STRAFFORD
No,
Why, no. I would not touch on that, the first.
I left you that. Well, Hollis?
. . . . Say at once
The King could find no time to set me free!
A mask at Theobald's?

HOLLIS
Hush . . . no such affair
Detains him.

STRAFFORD
True: what needs so great a matter?
The Queen's lip may be sore!—Well: when he pleases,—
Only, I want the air: it vexes one
To be pent up so long!

HOLLIS
The King . . . I bear
His message, Strafford . . . pray you, let me speak!

STRAFFORD
Go, William! Anne, try o'er your song again!

[The **CHILDREN** retire.

They shall be loyal, friend, at all events.
I know your message: you have nothing new
To tell me: from the first I guessed as much.
I know, instead of coming here at once—
Leading me forth before them by the hand,—
I know the King will leave the door ajar
As though I were escaping . . . let me fly
While the mob gapes upon some show prepared

On the other side of the river!

HOLLIS [to his **COMPANION**]
Tell him all;
I knew my throat would thicken thus . . .Speak, you!

STRAFFORD
'Tis all one—I forgive him. Let me have
The order of release!
. . . I've heard, as well,
Of certain poor manoeuvrings to avoid
The granting pardon at his proper risk;
First, he must prattle somewhat to the Lords—
Must talk a trifle with the Commons first—
Be grieved I should abuse his confidence,
And far from blaming them, and . . .
. . . Where's the order?

HOLLIS
Spare me!

STRAFFORD
Why . . . . he'd not have me steal away?
—With an old doublet and a steeple hat
Like Prynne's? Be smuggled into France, perhaps?
Hollis, 'tis for my children! 'Twas for them
I e'er consented to stand day by day
And give those Puritans the best of words—
Be patient—speak when called upon—observe
Their rules,—and not give all of them the lie!

HOLLIS
No—Strafford . . .no escape . . .no . . .dearest Strafford!

STRAFFORD
What's in that boy of mine that he should be
Son to a prison-breaker? I shall stay
And he'll stay with me. Charles should know as much—
He too has children!
[Turning to **HOLLIS'S COMPANION**]
Ah, you feel for me!
No need to hide that face! Though it have looked
Upon me from the judgment-seat . . . I know
Strangely, that somewhere it has looked on me . . .
Still there is One who does not come—there's One
That shut out Heaven from me . . .

HOLLIS

Think on it then!
On Heaven . . .and calmly . . .as one . . .as one to die!

STRAFFORD
Die? True, friend, all must die, and all must need
Forgiveness: I forgive him from my soul.

HOLLIS
Be constant, now . . . be grand and brave . . be now
Just as when . . . Oh, I cannot stay for words . . .
'Tis a world's wonder . . .but . . .but . . .you must die!

STRAFFORD
Sir, if your errand is to set me free
This heartless jest will . . .
Hollis—you turn white,
And your lip shivers!—What if . . .
Oh, we'll end,
We'll end this! See this paper—warm . . feel . . warm
With lying next my heart! Whose hand is there?
Whose promise? Read! Read loud! For God to hear!
"Strafford shall take no hurt" . . .read it, I say!
"In person, honour, nor estate" . . . .

HOLLIS
The King . . .

STRAFFORD
I could unking him by a breath! You sit
Where Loudon sate . . .Loudon, who came to tell
The certain end, and offer me Pym's pardon
If I'd forsake the King—and I stood firm
On my King's faith! The King who lived . . .

HOLLIS
To sign
The warrant for your death.

STRAFFORD
"Put not your trust
In Princes, neither in the sons of men,
In whom is no salvation!" On that King—
Upon his head . . .

CHARLES
O Hollis, he will curse me!

HOLLIS

The scaffold is prepared—they wait for you—
He has consented . . .

CHARLES
No, no—stay first—Strafford!
You would not see me perish at your foot . . .
It was wrung from me! Only curse me not!
The Queen had cruel eyes! And Vane declared . . .
And I believed I could have rescued you . . .
Strafford—they threaten me! and . . .well, speak now,
And let me die!—

HOLLIS [To **STRAFFORD**]
As you hope grace from God,
Be merciful to this most wretched man!

VOICES FROM WITHIN
Verso la sera
Di Primavera.

STRAFFORD [after a pause]
You'll be good to those children, Sire? I know
You'll not believe her even should the Queen
Think they take after one they never saw!
I had intended that my son should live
A stranger to these matters . . . but you are
So utterly deprived of friends! He too
Must serve you—will you not be good to him?
Stay—Sire—stay—do not promise—do not swear!
And, Hollis—do the best you can for me!
I've not a soul to trust to: Wandesford's dead—
And you've got Radcliffe safe—and Laud is here . .
I've had small time of late for my affairs—
But I'll trust any of you . . . Pym himself—
No one could hurt them: there's an infant, too—
. . . These tedious cares! Your Majesty could spare them—
But 'tis so awkward—dying in a hurry!
. . . Nay—Pardon me, my King! I had forgotten
Your education, trials, and temptations
And weakness . . I have said a peevish word—
But, mind I bless you at the last! You know
'Tis between you and me . . . what has the world
To do with it? Farewell!

CHARLES [at the door]
Balfour! Balfour!
. . . What, die? Strafford to die? This Strafford here?
Balfour! . . Nay Strafford, do not speak . . Balfour!

[Enter **BALFOUR**.

The Parliament . . . go to them—I grant all
Demands! Their sittings shall be permanent—
Tell them to keep their money if they will . . .
I'll come to them for every coat I wear
And every crust I eat, only I choose
To pardon Strafford—Strafford—my brave friend!

BALFOUR [aside]
Is he mad, Hollis?

CHARLES
Strafford, now, to die!
. . .But the Queen . . . ah, the Queen!—make haste, Balfour!
—You never heard the people howl for blood,
Beside!

BALFOUR
Your Majesty may hear them now:
The walls can hardly keep their murmurs out:
Please you retire!

CHARLES
Take all the troops, Balfour!

BALFOUR
There are some hundred thousand of the crowd.

CHARLES
Come with me, Strafford! You'll not fear them friend!

STRAFFORD
Balfour, say nothing to the world of this!
I charge you, as a dying man, forget
You gazed upon this agony of one . . .
Of one . . .or if . . .why you may say, Balfour,
The King was sorry—very—'tis no shame!
Yes, you may say he even wept, Balfour,—
And that I walked the lighter to the block
Because of it. I shall walk lightly, Sire!
—For I shall save you . . .save you at the last!
Earth fades, Heaven dawns on me . . .I shall wake next
Before God's throne: the moment's close at hand
When Man the first, last time, has leave to lay
His whole heart bare before its Maker—leave
To clear up the long error of a life

And choose one happiness for evermore.
With all mortality about me, Charles,
The sudden wreck—the dregs—the violent death . . .
I'll pray for you! Thro' all the Angel-song
Shall penetrate one weak and quivering prayer—
I'll say how good you are . . .inwardly good
And pure . .

[The **KING** falls: **HOLLIS** raises him.

Be witness, he could not prevent
My death! I'll go—ere he awakes—go now!
All must be ready—did you say, Balfour,
The crowd began to murmur?—They'll be kept
Too late for sermon at St. Antholin's!
Now—but tread softly—children are at play
In the next room—Ah, just my children—Hollis!
—Or . . . no—support the King!

[A door is unbarred.

Hark . . they are here!
Stay Hollis!—Go Balfour! I'll follow . . . . .

CARLISLE [Entering with many **ATTENDANTS**]
Me!
Follow me, Strafford, and be saved! . . . The King?
[To the **KING**]
Well—as you ordered . . .They are ranged without. . .
The convoy. . .

[Seeing the **KING'S** state.

[To **STRAFFORD**]
You know all then! Why, I thought
It looked so well that Charles should save you—Charles
Alone . . .'tis shame that you should owe it me—
Me . . .no, not shame! Strafford, you'll not feel shame
At being saved by me?

HOLLIS
All true! Oh Strafford,
She saves you! all her deed. . . this girl's own deed
—And is the boat in readiness? . . . You, friend,
Are Billingsley, no doubt! Speak to her, Strafford!
See how she trembles. . . waiting for your voice!
The world's to learn its bravest story yet!

CARLISLE
Talk afterward! Long nights in France enough
To sit beneath the vines and talk of home!

STRAFFORD
You love me, girl! . . . . Ah, Strafford can be loved
As well as Vane! I could escape, then?

CARLISLE
Haste. . .
Advance the torches, Bryan!

STRAFFORD
I will die!
They call me proud. . . but England had no right
When she encountered me—her strength to mine—
To find the chosen foe a craven! Girl,
I fought her to the utterance—I fell—
I am hers now. . . and I will die! Beside
The lookers-on! Eliot is all about
This place with his most uncomplaining brow!

CARLISLE
Strafford!

STRAFFORD
I think if you could know how much
I love you, you would be repaid, my girl!

CARLISLE
Then, for my sake!

STRAFFORD
Even for your sweet sake. . .
I stay.

HOLLIS
For their sake!

STRAFFORD
I bequeath a stain . . .
Leave me! Girl, humour me and let me die!

HOLLIS
No way to draw him hence—Carlisle—no way?

CARLISLE [Suddenly to **CHARLES**]
Bid him escape . . .wake, King! Bid him escape!

STRAFFORD [Looks earnestly at him]
Yes, I will go! Die, and forsake the King?
I'll not draw back from the last service.

CARLISLE
Strafford!

STRAFFORD
And, after all, what is disgrace to me?
Let us come, girl! . . . That it should end this way!
Lead then . . . but I feel strangely . . . it was not
To end this way!

CHARLES
Lean—lean on me!

STRAFFORD
My King!
Oh, had he trusted me—his Friend of friends—
Had he but trusted me!

CARLISLE
Leave not the king—
I can support him, Hollis!

STRAFFORD [Starting as they approach the door at the back]
Not this way;
This gate . . . I dreamed of it . . . this very gate!

CARLISLE
It opens on the river—our good boat
Is moored below—our friends are there!

STRAFFORD
The same!
Only with something ominous and dark,
Fatal, inevitable . . .

CARLISLE
Strafford! Strafford!

STRAFFORD
Not by this gate . . . I feel it will be there!
I dreamed of it, I tell you . . .touch it not!

CARLISLE
To save the King,—Strafford, to save the King!

[As **STRAFFORD** opens the door, **PYM** is discovered with **HAMPDEN**, **VANE**, &c. **STRAFFORD** falls back to the front of the stage: **PYM** follows slowly and confronts him.

PYM
Have I done well? Speak, England! Whose great sake
I still have laboured for, with disregard
To my own heart,—for whom my youth was made
Barren, my future dark, to offer up
Her sacrifice—this man, this Wentworth here—
That walked in youth with me—loved me it may be,
And whom, for his forsaking England's cause,
I hunted by all means (trusting that she
Would sanctify all means) even to the grave
That yawns for him. And saying this, I feel
No bitter pang than first I felt, the hour
I swore that Wentworth might leave us,—but I
Would never leave him: I do leave him now!
I render up my charge (be witness, God!)
To England who imposed it! I have done
Her bidding—poorly, wrongly,—it may be
With ill effects—for I am but a man. . . . .
Still, I have done my best, my very best,
Not faltering for a moment! I have done!

[After a pause.

And that said, I will say . . . yes, I will say
I never loved but this man—David not
More Jonathan! Even thus, I love him now:
And look for my chief portion in that world
Where great hearts led astray are turned again,
(Soon it may be . . .and . . .yes . . .it will be soon:
My mission over, I shall not live long!)—
. . . Aye here I know I talk—and I will talk
Of England—and her great reward—as all
I look for there; but in my inmost heart
Believe I think of stealing quite away
To walk once more with Wentworth—with my friend
Purged from all error, gloriously renewed,
And Eliot shall not blame us! Then indeed . .
(This is no meeting, Wentworth! Tears rise up
Too hot . . .A thin mist—is it blood?—enwraps
The face I loved so!) Then, shall the meeting be!
Then—then—then—I may kiss that hand, I know!

STRAFFORD [Walks calmly up to **PYM** and offers his hand]
I have loved England too; we'll meet then, Pym!

As well to die! Youth is the time—our youth,
To think and to decide on a great course:
Age with its action follows; but 'tis dreary
To have to alter one's whole life in age—
The time past, the strength gone! as well die now.
When we meet, Pym, I'd be set right—not now!
I'd die as I have lived . . .too late to change!
Best die. Then if there's any fault, it will
Be smothered up: much best! You'll be too busy
With your hereafter, you will have achieved
Too many triumphs to be always dwelling
Upon my downfall, Pym? Poor little Laud
May dream his dream out of a perfect Church
In some blind corner? And there's no one left . . .

[He glances on the **KING**.

I trust the King now wholly to you, Pym!
And yet . . . I know not! What if with this weakness . . .
And I shall not be there . . . And he'll betray
His friends—if he has any . . . And he's false . .
And loves the Queen, and. . .
Oh, my fate is nothing—
Nothing! But not that awful head. . . not that!

Pym, save the King! Pym, save him! Stay—you shall . . .
For you love England! I, that am dying, think
What I must see. . . 'tis here. . . all here! My God!
Let me but gasp out, in one word of fire,
How Thou wilt plague him, satiating Hell!
What? England that you love—our land—become
A green and putrefying charnel, left
Our children . . . some of us have children, Pym—
Some who, without that, still must ever wear
A darkened brow, an over-serious look,
And never properly be young . . .
No word!
You will not say a word—to me—to Him!

[Turning to **CHARLES**.

Speak to him . . . as you spoke to me . . . that day!
Nay, I will let you pray to him, my King—
Pray to him! He will kiss your feet, I know!

What if I curse you? Send a strong Curse forth
Clothed from my heart, lapped round with horror, till
She's fit, with her white face, to walk the world

Scaring kind natures from your cause and you—
Then to sit down with you, at the board-head,
The gathering for prayer. . . .

VANE
O speak, Pym! Speak!

STRAFFORD
. . . Creep up, and quietly follow each one home—
You—you—you—be a nestling Care for each
To sleep with, hardly moaning in his dreams . . .
She gnaws so quietly . . . until he starts—
Gets off with half a heart eaten away . . .
Oh you shall 'scape with less, if she's my child!

VANE [To **PYM**]
We never thought of this . . . surely not dreamed
Of this . . .it never can . . . could come to this!

PYM [After a pause]
If England should declare her will to me . . .

STRAFFORD
No—not for England, now—not for Heaven, now . . .
See, Pym—for me! My sake! I kneel to you!
There . . .I will thank you for the death . . . my friend,
This is the meeting . . . you will send me proud
To my chill grave! Dear Pym—I'll love you well!
Save him for me, and let me love you well!

PYM
England—I am thine own! Dost thou exact
That service? I obey thee to the end!

STRAFFORD [as he totters out]
O God, I shall die first—I shall die first!

Robert Browning – A Short Biography

He is the equal of any Victorian Poet that could be mentioned. However, Browning continues to be in the shadow of Tennyson, Arnold, Hopkins, Morris and many others.

Robert Browning was born on May 7th, 1812 in Walworth in the parish of Camberwell, London. He was baptized on June 14th, 1812, at Lock's Fields Independent Chapel, York Street, Walworth.

Browning's early years were certainly very interesting. His mother was an excellent pianist and a very devout evangelical Christian. His father, who worked as a clerk at the Bank of England, was also an artist, scholar, antiquarian, and collector of books and pictures. Indeed, he amassed more than 6,000 volumes of rare books including works in Greek, Hebrew, Latin, French, Italian, and Spanish. For the young and curious Browning, it was a wonderful resource, added to which his father was a guiding force in his education.

Many accounts attest that Browning was already proficient at reading and writing by the age of five. He is said to have been a bright but anxious student and to have studied and learnt Latin, Greek, and French by the time he was fourteen. From fourteen to sixteen he was educated at home, tutored in music, drawing, dancing, and horsemanship. Certainly, language and the arts were two areas the young Browning both absorbed and pushed himself towards.

At the age of twelve he wrote a volume of Byronic verse he called Incondita, which his parents attempted to have published. The attempts were unsuccessful and, disappointed, Browning destroyed the work.

In 1825, a cousin gave Browning a collection of Percy Bysshe Shelley's poetry; Browning was so enamored with the poems that he asked for the rest of Shelley's works for his thirteenth birthday. In fact, Browning then went the extra mile, declaring himself to be both a vegetarian and an atheist in honour of his hero.

Intriguingly it seems that the rejection of his first volume didn't dim his appreciation of other poets, but it appears to have stopped him writing any poems between the ages of thirteen and twenty.

In 1828, Browning enrolled at the newly-opened University of London. He was uncomfortable with the experience and he soon left, anxious to read and absorb at his own pace.

His education which, overall is notably rambling and lacks a structure that many of his artistic contemporaries enjoyed, i.e. excellent public schooling and then a degree at Oxford or Cambridge, may present many of his critics with ammunition to criticize, but alternatively his hap-hazard education certainly contributed to many of the references that baffled both critics and his audience, but they tellingly show the breath and scale of what he could turn words too. What others would call obscure references were, to Browning, remarkably obvious.

Browning's early career was very promising. His long poem Pauline (of which only a fragment was ever finished and published) brought him to the attention of the Pre-Raphaelite master Dante Gabriel Rossetti and his difficult Paracelsus (published in 1835) was warmly admired by both Dickens and Wordsworth.

In the 1830s he met the actor William Macready and was encouraged to develop and turn his talents to the stage by writing verse drama. But these plays, including Strafford, which ran for five nights in 1837, and those contained within the Bells and Pomegranates series, were, for the most part, unsuccessful.

During this period Browning began to discover that his real talents lay in taking a single character and allowing that character to discover more about himself by revealing further personal aspects of himself in his speeches; the dramatic monologue. The techniques he developed through this—especially the use of diction, rhythm, and symbol—are regarded as his most important contribution to poetry. They would later influence such major poets of the 20th Century as Ezra Pound, T. S. Eliot, and Robert Frost.

By 1840, with the publication of Sordello, the tide turned somewhat. Many thought he was being deliberately obscure, opaque beyond measure and his poetry for the next decade or so was not eagerly acquired or talked about.

As Browning attempted to rehabilitate his career he began a relationship with Elizabeth Barrett in 1845. He had read her poems and, being totally charmed by their quality, was determined to meet her. The poetess was better known than the younger Browning but suffered from a debilitating illness and was also subject to the harsh behaviour of her over-bearing father. Nevertheless, the new couple were soon inseparable.

Her father, as he did with any of his children that married, disinherited her. Despite this she had some money from her own resources and sensing that the best outcome for both the relationship and her own health was to move abroad the couple did just that. After a private marriage at St Marylebone Parish Church, in September 1846, they journeyed to Europe to honeymoon in Paris.

Their new life now took them to Italy, first to Pisa and a little later to Florence. There they absorbed life and one another.

But in the short term the literary assault on Browning's work did not let up. He was now criticized by such patrician writers as Charles Kingsley for his abandonment of England for foreign lands. Browning could do little to answer these attacks except to compose with his pen and continue with his poetical journey.

The Browning's were well respected, and even famous. Elizabeth health began to improve, she grew stronger and in 1849, at the age of 43, between four miscarriages, she gave birth to a son, Robert Wiedeman Barrett Browning, whom they nicknamed "Penini" or "Pen",

Intriguingly despite his growing reputation and return to form as a poet he was more often than not known as 'Elizabeth Barrett's husband'.

Work flowed from his pen that was to ensure his reputation as one of England's leading poets. When his collection Men and Women was published in 1855 it contained some of his finest lines. It was dedicated to Elizabeth. Life had begun to smile handsome rewards upon the Brownings.

Victorian society was very much taken with all things spiritualist. It was not enough to have command of much of the globe through Empire, they wished to know and explore wherever they could. The spirit world beckoned their interest. Browning dissented from this view believing it was all a hoax and a fraud. Elizabeth, however, was inclined to believe and this caused several disagreements between the couple.

They attended a séance by Daniel Dunglas Home, in July 1855. (Home was a famous and clamored after Scottish physical medium with the reported ability to levitate and speak with the dead). It is said that during this séance a spirit face materialised. Home then claimed it was the face of Browning's son who had died in infancy. Browning seized the 'materialisation' which turned out to be Home's bare foot. Browning had never lost a son in infancy.

After the séance, Browning wrote an angry letter to The Times, in which he said: "the whole display of hands, spirit utterances etc., was a cheat and imposture."

The Browning's time in Italy were immensely rewarding years for both their personal and professional lives. Browning encouraged her to include Sonnets from the Portuguese in her published works, these beautiful poems are undoubtedly one of the highlights of English love poetry.

Elizabeth had become quite politicised during these years. Engrossed in Italian politics (which was continuing to slowly re-unify the country), she issued a small volume of political poems entitled Poems before Congress (1860) most of which were written to express her sympathy with the Italian cause after the earlier outbreak of The Second Italian Independence War in 1859. In England they caused uproar. Conservative magazines such as Blackwood's and the Saturday Review labelled her a fanatic. She dedicated the book to her husband.

But in 1861 tragedy struck.

The couple had spent the winter of 1860–61 in Rome when Elizabeth's health deteriorated again and they returned to Florence in early June. However, these turned out to be her final weeks. Only morphine would now still the pain. She died in Browning's arms on June 29th, 1861. Browning said that she died "smilingly, happily, and with a face like a girl's .... Her last word was .... "Beautiful".

Her burial took place in the nearby Protestant English Cemetery of Florence. The local people were deeply saddened, and shops closed their doors in grief and respect.

Browning and their son were obviously devastated. Unable to bear being in Florence without Elizabeth they soon returned to London to live at 19 Warwick Crescent, Maida Vale.

As he re-integrated himself back into the London literary scene he began to finally receive the proper praise, respect and reputation that his works deserved.

Browning went on to publish Dramatis Personæ (1864), and The Ring and the Book (1868–1869). The latter, based on an "old yellow book" which told of a seventeenth-century Italian murder trial, received wide and generous critical acclaim. Although by now he was in the twilight of a long and prolific career, that had achieved some notable ups and downs, he was respected and indeed renowned for his talents and works.

In 1878, he revisited Italy for the first time since Elizabeth's death. He would return there on several further occasions but never to Florence.

Such was the esteem he was held in that The Browning Society was founded in 1881. Although he had never obtained a degree (something that set him apart from many other Victorian poets) he was now awarded honorary degrees from Oxford University in 1882 and then the University of Edinburgh in 1884.

In 1887, Browning produced the major work of his later years, Parleyings with Certain People of Importance in Their Day. Browning now spoke with his own voice as he engaged in a series of dialogues with long-forgotten figures of literary, artistic, and philosophic history. Unfortunately, both the critics and public were completely baffled by this.

On April 7th, 1889 Browning attended a dinner party at the home of his friend, the artist Rudolf Lehmann. The highlight of which was a recording made on a wax cylinder on an Edison cylinder phonograph. On the recording, which still exists, Browning recites part of How They Brought the Good News from Ghent to Aix, and can even be heard apologising when he forgets the words.

The recording was first played in 1890 on the anniversary of his death, at a gathering of his admirers, it was said to be the first time anyone's voice 'had been heard from beyond the grave'.

His last work Asolando: Fancies and Facts (1889), returned to his brief and concise lyric verse that was so popular. It was published on the day of his death on December 12th, 1889, Robert Browning was at his son's home Ca' Rezzonico in Venice.

He was buried in Poets' Corner in Westminster Abbey; his grave lies immediately adjacent to that of Alfred Tennyson.

Among the many who have publicly acknowledged their literary debt to him are Henry James, Oscar Wilde, George Bernard Shaw, G. K. Chesterton, Ezra Pound, Jorge Luis Borges, and Vladimir Nabokov.

Robert Browning - A Concise Bibliography

Here follows a list of the plays and poetry volumes published during his lifetime. Poems of particular worth are noted from within those volumes.

Pauline: A Fragment of a Confession (1833)
Paracelsus (1835)
Strafford (play) (1837)
Sordello (1840)
Bells and Pomegranates No. I: Pippa Passes (play) (1841)
    The Year's at the Spring
Bells and Pomegranates No. II: King Victor and King Charles (play) (1842)
Bells and Pomegranates No. III: Dramatic Lyrics (1842)
    Porphyria's Lover
    Soliloquy of the Spanish Cloister
    My Last Duchess
    The Pied Piper of Hamelin
    Count Gismond
    Johannes Agricola in Meditation
Bells and Pomegranates No. IV: The Return of the Druses (play) (1843)
Bells and Pomegranates No. V: A Blot in the 'Scutcheon (play) (1843)
Bells and Pomegranates No. VI: Colombe's Birthday (play) (1844)
Bells and Pomegranates No. VII: Dramatic Romances and Lyrics (1845)
    The Laboratory
    How They Brought the Good News from Ghent to Aix
    The Bishop Orders His Tomb at Saint Praxed's Church
    The Lost Leader
    Home Thoughts from Abroad

      Meeting at Night
Bells and Pomegranates No. VIII: Luria and A Soul's Tragedy (plays) (1846)
Christmas-Eve and Easter-Day (1850)
An Essay on Percy Bysshe Shelley (essay) (1852)
Two Poems (1854)
Men and Women (1855)
      Love Among the Ruins
      A Toccata of Galuppi's
      Childe Roland to the Dark Tower Came
      Fra Lippo Lippi
      Andrea Del Sarto
      The Patriot
      The Last Ride Together
      Memorabilia
      Cleon
      How It Strikes a Contemporary
      The Statue and the Bust
      A Grammarian's Funeral
      An Epistle Containing the Strange Medical Experience of Karshish, the Arab Physician
      Bishop Blougram's Apology
      Master Hugues of Saxe-Gotha
      By the Fire-side
Dramatis Personae (1864)
      Caliban upon Setebos
      Rabbi Ben Ezra
      Abt Vogler
      Mr. Sludge, "The Medium"
      Prospice
      A Death in the Desert
The Ring and the Book (1868–69)
Balaustion's Adventure (1871)
Prince Hohenstiel-Schwangau, Saviour of Society (1871)
Fifine at the Fair (1872)
Red Cotton Night-Cap Country, or, Turf and Towers (1873)
Aristophanes' Apology (1875)
      Thamuris Marching
The Inn Album (1875)
Pacchiarotto, and How He Worked in Distemper (1876)
      Numpholeptos
The Agamemnon of Aeschylus (1877)
La Saisiaz and The Two Poets of Croisic (1878)
Dramatic Idylls (1879)
Dramatic Idylls: Second Series (1880)
      Pan and Luna
Jocoseria (1883)
Ferishtah's Fancies (1884)
Parleyings with Certain People of Importance in Their Day (1887)
Asolando (1889)

www.ingramcontent.com/pod-product-compliance
Lightning Source LLC
Chambersburg PA
CBHW060122050426
42448CB00010B/1993